Val

Horse Problems and Vices Explained

WARD LOCK LIMITED · LONDON

Horseman's Handbooks

TRAINING EXPLAINED
JUMPING EXPLAINED
STABLE MANAGEMENT EXPLAINED
DRESSAGE EXPLAINED
TACK EXPLAINED
SHOWDRIVING EXPLAINED
SHOWING AND RINGCRAFT EXPLAINED
HORSES' HEALTH SIMPLIFIED
LONG DISTANCE RIDING EXPLAINED
HORSE AND PONY BREEDING EXPLAINED
BASIC RIDING EXPLAINED
ALL ABOUT YOUR PONY

We are very grateful to John Elliott for kindly providing the photographs for this book and for the back cover; to Margaret Herring for the photograph on page 77 and the front cover; to Nils Solberg for the line drawings; and to Alison Sherred for the Glossary of US equivalents.

First published in Great Britain in 1982
by Ward Lock Limited, 82 Gower Street,
London WC1E 6EQ, an Egmont Company.
Reprinted 1985

House editor Suzanna Osman Jones

Text set in Times
by Presentia Art, Horsham, UK

Printed and bound in Great Britain by Hollen Street Press, Slough

British Library Cataloguing in Publication Data

Ledger, Val
  Horse problems and vices explained. – (Horseman's handbooks)
  1. Horses – Behaviour
  I. Title II. Series
  636.1 SF281
  ISBN 0-7063-6411-2

Contents

Horses are very responsive to tone in the human voice. Their mobile ears can be directed towards a sound, besides expressing the horse's own mood.

1 Introduction - understanding your horse

In the following chapters on vices and bad habits found in horses and ponies, I have suggested some ways of trying to correct them. First, there are some facts about equine behaviour patterns that should be kept in mind.

These days, horses are meant to be a source of pleasure to us, since we no longer rely on them as working animals; their willingness to co-operate has allowed them to be domesticated for our use and enjoyment. If we are to enjoy them, it is only fair that they should not have to 'suffer' us.

Horses are what we make of them, or unfortunately, what other people have made of them before they come to us. Our own actions, and whether they are sympathetic or thoughtless, will strongly affect our horses' behaviour towards us. Where a sympathetic trainer can nearly always produce a kind and co-operative horse, a careless or cruel trainer may produce one who is nervous and timid or worse still, vicious.

Before you can set out to cure a vice or bad habit, you must first ascertain the cause and decide whether it is partially or wholly justified. Most problems, with young horses particularly, begin with the horse misunderstanding what is being asked of him. If the trainer is impatient he will end up by confusing his horse, and more serious, may punish him unduly for apparent lack of co-operation. It is of the utmost importance, when handling and schooling horses, for the trainer to ascertain whether a horse's unwillingness to co-operate is the result of fear or misunderstanding, or true disobedience. Nothing is more damaging to a horse's education than his losing his trust in his trainer, which he will if he is afraid and misunderstands what is required. This merely gives rise to confusion, and the bond of trust and friendship he offers us will begin to disintegrate.

Communicating with horses

It is a sad fact that so many riders, trainers and grooms do not cultivate their horses' intelligence, so they fail to communicate properly with them, through lack of knowledge of horses' powers of understanding. The horse has little or no power of actual reasoning; the simplest form of communication with him works on a basis of 'association of ideas'. For example – horses like carrots, so if you take your horse a carrot when you go to catch him he will associate being caught with something he enjoys – the carrot. On the other hand, if he plays up when you go to catch him and you shout and chase him and then punish him when you do eventually catch him, he will associate being caught with being punished. You can guess the result; very soon you will have a horse you cannot catch at all. Although I do not believe in bribing horses to co-operate, there are times when a simple reward is worth a great deal towards cementing their trust and friendship. This is the first step towards any successful partnership between horse and rider; without it you cannot begin to enjoy a happy relationship.

Horses learn quickly if taught properly, and the best way to instil a lesson into their minds is by repetition. However, you must keep the lessons short, especially with youngsters, as horses do not usually concentrate for long periods and they quickly become bored doing the same thing over and over again. It is much better to achieve a little done well, than to over-extend a lesson, create more problems by boring or confusing the horse and have to end on a bad note. If you handle your horse correctly and allow him to enjoy his schooling, he will be keen and respond willingly to try to please you.

It is worth remembering that horses have very sensitive hearing and are often upset by loud noises and loud voices. A number of horses will not behave kindly when handled by men, but are models of good behaviour when looked after by women, and this may be attributable to the different tones of voice. Generally, people do not seem to talk to their horses enough. Some tend to keep a sacred silence even when riding, but use of the voice is probably the most valuable form of communication that there is between horse and man, and it should be used widely.

We can read our horse's mood and wishes very clearly from his facial expressions, but he cannot do the same with us. He can however, easily interpret our moods and wishes from our tone of voice. When we are pleased, our voices lift a little and sound musical

First establish a friendly, trusting relationship with your horse.

from the sing-song lilt of our words. (Try saying 'There's a good lad', out loud to yourself and you will see what is meant.) When we are annoyed, the voice will become raised and harsh; when we are trying to soothe the horse the voice will become soft and low. The need for communication is obvious; its level of efficiency can be greatly increased by practising methodical use of the voice. Shouting at a horse will only upset him and is unlikely to enhance his co-operation.

While it is important to be endlessly patient and kind, especially with young horses, the trainer must nevertheless always be firm. What may appear at first to be a bit of high spirits can very soon turn into a nasty habit if not checked immediately. For instance – never allow a youngster to nip you without giving him a reminder, and

7

never fall into the trap of giving horses and ponies titbits regularly; nothing leads more quickly to the habit of biting than this. If your horse knows you have titbits in your pocket and he is accustomed to being given some every time he nuzzles your coat, you cannot expect him not to be annoyed if you do not give him some every time he 'asks' for some. Bad habits are much easier to prevent than to cure. A little thought can prevent a great deal of trouble and unnecessary misery for both you and your horse.

Boredom and bad habits
Most bad habits are caused by boredom – the usual result of inactivity. While this may occasionally be on account of an injury which results in the horse being stabled twenty-four hours per day, it is more often the result of bad management, particularly of young horses. Lack of exercise in a fit young horse can quickly lead to the acquisition of a number of stable vices, i.e., door-banging, rug-tearing, weaving, and so on. It is significant that a horse who lives in may spend twenty-two hours in every twenty-four confined to a very small area, with only his feeding and grooming periods to break up the monotony. Bearing in mind that this situation is so different from a horse's natural behaviour pattern, that of a free-ranging animal, it is not surprising that it can lead to the frustration which causes stable vices. Whilst our horses are mostly bred in captivity and are domesticated animals, their basic instincts still remain to a certain extent, and must be catered for whenever possible.

Boredom of this kind should be easy to prevent by regular and sufficient exercise, coupled with careful feeding to ensure that the horse is not overfed and thereby suffering from a great surplus of energy. Most horses enjoy being turned out to pasture; while this may mean a good deal of extra work and take up time, it is a small price to pay to prevent boredom and bad habits from starting.

When to use punishment
A vital word of warning about punishment – before you correct your horse for being uncooperative or disobedient, first ask yourself 'Why did he do that?', or 'Why won't he do this?' If the answer is that he does not understand or is frightened or confused, then it is your reassurance and confidence that he needs, not impatience. Only if you are sure that your horse fully understands you, and is being purely disobedient, are you justified in punishing him, and then only

fairly. Never lose your temper. Sometimes it is not easy when you know he is being plain disobedient, which is usually when he has you at your worst disadvantage, but you must nevertheless be fair with him. If you are unfair, he may well learn to retaliate.

Being fair always is the only way to win a horse's respect. Your actions should be deliberate but always gentle and your attitude firm but not authoritative. If you are frightened of the horse he will know and take advantage of it, so you must be bold, not hesitant. Nor must you overreact if he misbehaves, as unfair handling will only aggravate the problems. Only one of you can be in command of the situation, and it must of course be you and not the horse.

The 'pecking order'

Being in command is really a question of establishing yourself in the 'pecking order'. When a number of horses are turned out together in the field, there is a distinct 'pecking order' between them. One horse will elect to be the 'boss' and will stay the 'boss' unless challenged and overcome; the others will be in a descending line of subservience beneath him. The one in the middle of a group of seven horses will show respect to his three superiors, and command respect himself from the other three whom he can boss around. It is up to you to make sure your horse realizes that you are most definitely his superior, and that any attempt to challenge your position in the 'pecking order' will be severely reprimanded. Although we are physically inferior to horses, we are mentally superior, and for this reason we can command respect. The moment that they realize they are physically superior is when trouble begins; so they should never be allowed to step out of line or use any kind of threatening behaviour without being reminded of who is the 'boss'.

2 Problems and vices in the stable

Door-banging

Door-banging is a bad habit that is not recognized as an unsoundness in a horse, but it can most definitely cause it. As well as being most annoying, it can damage the stable in time.

If it is confined to feeding times, it is just about tolerable, but incessant door-banging can be very tiresome. A horse will bang with either his knees or his feet, and big knees, or at least sore knees can result, and a variety of bone troubles can be triggered off by the excessive concussion received by the wall of the foot. In either case, the horse can easily lame himself.

A horse usually bangs for one of the following reasons – firstly, he may discover that this is a means of getting attention, and then it becomes a habit. When he first tried it he may have been given some hay in an attempt to appease him; this procedure of banging followed by being given hay served to teach him that he could be rewarded with food when he banged and so a bad habit developed. Secondly, horses who dislike being stabled may bang their doors as an objection to being kept in. Thirdly, and just as common a reason, is boredom.

Although it may be very easy to lose your temper with a horse who bangs incessantly, there is nothing to be gained from punishing him, for as soon as you go away, he will start to bang again. Hitting a horse over the stable door in unforgiveable; he may hurt himself if he throws up his head, and such treatment will only make him headshy.

If he only bangs at feeding times, be sure to feed him before the other horses; and in the same way, if he bangs when he sees the other horses being turned out and he is going out too, turn him out first. This way you will prevent him from banging to a certain extent.

If the horse is banging merely for the sake of getting attention and you ignore it early on, it is possible that he will give up the habit of his own accord.

There are a number of other things you can try to stop door-banging. One method is to fit a removable hollow metal bar into the door posts (*see* diagram). It should be situated at approximately 1.7m (5ft 6in) from the ground to be effective on a horse of 15 hands high. A hole should be drilled in each door post at the optimum height and a spring inserted into one end of the bar. The bar is then fitted, spring first, into one hole and the spring depressed until the other end of the bar can be eased into the hole opposite. It is important that the bar should be just longer than the width of the doorway, so that the spring is not exposed when the bar is fitted, otherwise it may be pushed out by the horse. Be sure to drill one of the holes sufficiently deep to allow the spring to be pushed well back when fitting the bar, which must be eased in, as it is slightly longer than the doorway is wide.

To determine the optimum height at which to fit the bar, it should be noted that the horse must only just be able to stand comfortably with his head over it. If he tries to bang the door in this position, he

A high bar fixed across the open top of the stable door to discourage door-banging. This can be a hollow metal bar with a spring at one end, or a slip rail. It should be able to be lifted out quickly when you want to take the horse out.

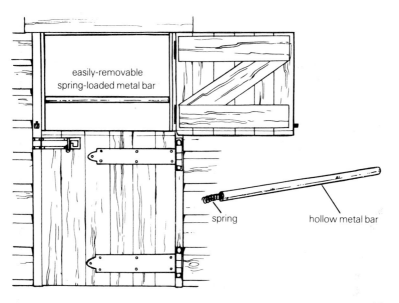

easily-removable spring-loaded metal bar

spring

hollow metal bar

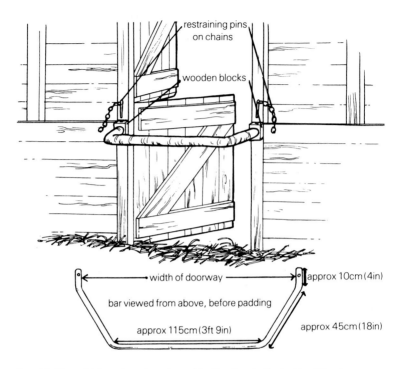

A padded bar which projects into the stable, fitted on to the inside of the door, an alternative discouragement to door-banging.

will find that the bar causes him discomfort by pressing on his throat. This will make him lift his head back over the door, and so prevent him from standing close enough to bang on it.

Alternatively, a metal bar can be fitted to the inside of the door at the approximate height of the horse's chest (*see* diagram) so that it projects into the stable to a distance of half a metre (20in) or so. This will prevent the horse from standing directly in front of the door and being able to strike it. The bar should be securely fitted into two blocks of wood which must be firmly attached to the two door posts. By drilling holes through the tops of the two blocks and corresponding holes through the bar at each end, the whole may be secured by passing a restraining pin through. This will be necessary so that the horse cannot pull it out. It should be well padded, to prevent him hurting himself. Foam rubber used for lagging pipes is suitable for this and can be bought ready moulded and slit open for easy fitting; should be covered with a suitable fabric such as Vinyl. If the horse tries to tear it with his teeth, applying a paste such as 'Cribox' will soon stop him.

A horse who bangs with his knees can be protected by wearing kneecaps whilst in the stable. These must be fitted correctly so as not to cause discomfort. Skeleton kneecaps are the best type – the ones with rugging around them will become very soiled when the horse lies down. Chamois lining inside the top strap is better than grain-side leather, as it is much softer so the padding will have more give. When fitting, take care to ensure that the top strap is tight enough, but not too tight. When fastened, it should be tight enough for the kneecap not to be pulled down over the knee. If this is possible, it is too loose. The bottom strap must not be done up tightly, but should be a fairly close fit, so that when the horse lies down, there is no possibility of him catching a foot in the strap on the opposite leg.

Another idea is to nail or screw a row of old dandy brushes (bristles towards you) to the inside of the door, at the level at which the horse bangs – which should be quite easy to determine by the marks on the inside of the door. This is mostly effective with horses who bang with their knees, as a row of brushes will not have much effect on the feet. A large stout piece of door-matting fixed to the inside of the door will minimize the concussion to the horse's feet, and cut down on the noise.

If none of these provides a solution, the use of a full-grille fitted to the lower door of the stable will prevent the horse from standing sufficiently near to it to bang. However, shutting horses into their boxes must be held as a last resort, as it makes them bored and fretful.

In common with most other stable vices, this habit is catching, so horses who bang should be kept from the sight of others in the yard. It is hard to imagine anything worse than a yard full of banging horses early every Sunday morning.

Crib-biting

The act of crib-biting is observed when a horse catches hold of his manger, haynet or similar object with his teeth and then sharply and noisily draws in air which is swallowed. This habit is virtually continuous, being performed at regular short intervals, as often as four or five times per minute in bad cases. It is a recognized vice.

13

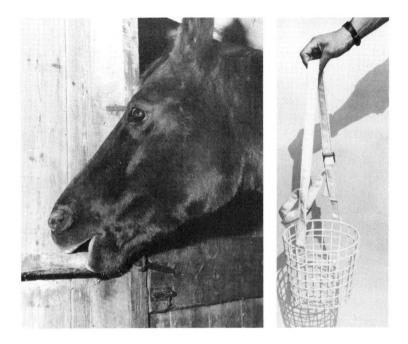

Left Simply cutting his teeth on a soft wood ledge in the stable, such as this one, can start a youngster off crib-biting.

Right A plastic covered wire muzzle with nylon headpiece and throatlatch is light, comfortable and hygienic and a horse may drink happily with it on.

Unfortunately the effect it has on the horse's health is manifold. His incisor teeth become badly damaged, the biting surfaces being worn down by constant contact with hard objects; this can lead to his being unable to graze properly.

The constant intake of air into the stomach, coupled with the habitual muscle contractions and grunting can lead easily to chronic digestive disorders and susceptibility to recurrent attacks of colic. Also, because the habit is continuous, the horse is hardly ever at rest, which can lead to loss of condition. In some cases, these side effects make it very difficult to keep flesh on the horse at all.

Another drawback is that it is difficult to tell the age of a crib-biter, due to the wearing down of the incisor teeth. They are also a 'dead giveaway' to any prospective buyer. Crib-biting is a recognized unsoundness, and as such renders a horse unable to be passed as 'sound' by a veterinary surgeon. This will seriously affect his value.

There are two common causes for crib-biting – mimicry of other horses and boredom. Horses will pass on such habits to one another very quickly and therefore it is very important that a horse with such a habit is kept out of sight of others. If he is not isolated it will not be long before every horse in the yard has picked up the vice. A significant factor is that most horses that crib-bite constantly whilst stabled, rarely continue the habit when turned out, but then take up where they left off as soon as they are brought in again.

Whilst it is incurable without using surgery, there are several things that can be done to alleviate this habit. To begin with, remove from the stable all projecting objects which the horse can seize with his teeth. This is not as difficult as it may appear. Haynets and hayracks can be dispensed with and hay fed loose on the floor of the box. Corner mangers must be removed, and feeds should be given in a feed tin, which must be removed once the horse has finished eating. Water buckets are the worst problem, for while they may be withdrawn from the stable during the day, and the horse watered regularly before feeding etc., they must, for obvious reasons be left in the stable at night. It is better, however, to substitute a suitable, thick-rimmed container for water, designed to prevent the horse seizing it with his teeth. Place the container on the ground, not at breast height, to discourage the horse from attempting to crib-bite on it.

By having a roller-bar fitted to the top of the stable door, you can prevent the horse taking a sufficient hold to crib on it. Any other projections in the box must be clad over with chipboard or thick plywood. If it is not possible to cover up everything, the application of creosote or such a proprietory brand paste as 'Cribox', which tastes nasty, will effect a cure in most cases. Any new wood, especially soft wood, introduced into a stable should be treated with a substance which will discourage a horse from chewing and biting it, as the availability of easily-chewed wood may itself lead to him becoming a crib-biter. A number of crib-biters also wind-suck (*see* next section).

You might think that an obvious way of preventing a horse from crib-biting is for him to wear a muzzle. However, this seemingly good idea has several drawbacks. The muzzle must be removed every time the horse is fed, and cannot be worn at night when he will have been given the bulk of his hay. Watering will also need to be monitored, as some horses will not drink when wearing a muzzle. Therefore the actual number of hours during which he can wear it is rather limited. If a muzzle is to be worn, it must be kept scrupulously clean, and plastic-covered wire muzzles are the easiest in this respect. Leather muzzles are more difficult and must not have too much saddle soap or oil applied to them as the horse has a very delicate sense of smell, and sensitive skin around his nose and lips which may be irritated. If he tries to drink whilst wearing a muzzle that has been recently oiled, the water will become oily, and this will put him off drinking it.

Anti-crib-biting bits are available on order from most good saddlers, but are expensive. They are usually effective, when fitted correctly, but as with the muzzle, their use is limited as they too must be removed for feeding, at night and so on.

As a cure, surgery used not to be recommended, but modern surgical techniques have advanced, and the procedure has been refined. It involves the removal of muscle used in arching the neck, and the nerve which serves the large muscles beneath the jugular vein. Scarring is minimal and the head carriage is not affected. The success rate is very high and the cost is not exhorbitant.

It goes without saying that to buy a horse that is a crib-biter is asking for all sorts of trouble. Great care should always be taken to see that no horse is given cause to pick up this serious vice.

Wind-sucking

Wind-sucking is a vice very similar to crib-biting, but differs in that it is not necessary for the horse to grasp an object with his teeth in order to do it. The causes are usually identical to those of crib-biting and the effects on the horse's health and value apply similarly.

It is obviously unnecessary to modify the stable as in the case of the crib-biter, but much can be done to effect a cure by alleviating boredom, which, in general, is the major cause.

It will be noted that, as with crib-biters, horses that wind-suck when stabled rarely continue it when turned out, but begin again once they are brought in. If it is possible for horses with this habit to live out all the time, or at least only be stabled at night, then the problem will be greatly reduced. Only a really suitable field will help, and this means a large field with adequate keep that will stimulate the horse's interest. A small bare paddock will see him standing by the gate, bored and wind-sucking.

16

The wind-sucking strap – this device may also effect a cure for the crib-biter.

A 'wind-sucking strap' can be bought from the saddler for the horse to wear whilst stabled. It is a wide leather strap which is fitted to and fastened around the top of the horse's neck, just behind the ears, to prevent him contracting the muscles used for wind-sucking. This device will only be effective and safe for the horse to wear if fitted correctly and expert advice should be sought if you decide to use it.

As with crib-biting, a permanent cure may be effected using the surgical technique outlined in the previous section. However, buying a horse that wind-sucks may be more trouble than the horse is worth, even if he is inexpensive – which will probably be due to the fact that he is a wind-sucker.

Weaving

A horse is said to be 'weaving', when he waves his head incessantly from side to side over the stable door, while at the same time, shifts his forehand weight alternatively from one forefoot to the other and back again. His appearance is one of frustration, and the continuous rocking motion is mentally and physically wearing for him. He will lose physical condition through the ceaseless movement. Weaving can cause a deterioration in his action by fatiguing the forehand muscles. This can cause stumbling when the horse is doing fast work, which is obviously going to be very dangerous. The actual strain of being forever on the move in this swaying action will also make him lose weight.

Weaving is usually caused by boredom in the stabled horse, but like other such vices, can easily be started by the imitation of a stable mate, so weavers must be kept out of sight of other horses, along with crib-biters and wind-suckers. Weaving also constitutes an

Left A made-to-measure, purpose-built half-grille which is firmly fixed on to the lower half of the stable door to prevent weaving. It can be made by a blacksmith. It is the most satisfactory prevention, but expensive.

Right Tie-logs hung over the top half of the stable doorway to discourage weaving. These are spherical wood blocks used in old-fashioned stalls, attached to the end of a rope which passed through a ring and was then attached to the horse's headcollar. They can be bought. Other wood blocks can be used but they must be smooth and without corners.

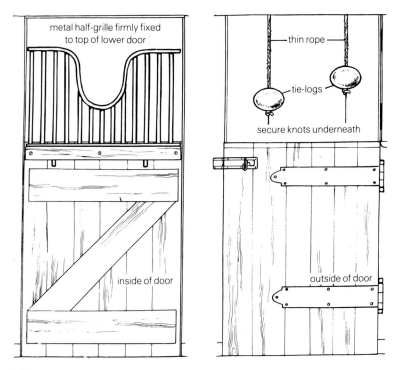

unsoundness for which a horse may be rejected by a veterinary surgeon, and for this reason he may also be returned to a vendor under a soundness warranty. It is a vice.

There is no actual cure, but it can be easily curtailed. If the cause is boredom, then turning the horse out into a field can alleviate it to some extent, and proper management of exercising and feeding routines will also be beneficial.

The best way to stop weaving in the stable is to construct a half-grille (*see* diagram) which can be fitted to the lower door. This is the most successful and safest means and it still allows the horse to put his head over the door and be able to see what is going on around him in the yard. Although both would work, to close the top door or put up a full grille would only frustrate him further. It would compound the original cause of his weaving, as he would be more bored than before.

It is worth remembering that the half-grille should be fitted to the lower door of the stable so that it will open with the door and not have to be removed and replaced whenever the horse is taken in and out of the box. If the grille is fitted to the stable walls, it will be a waste of effort and time to use it.

As a temporary measure, or where finance does not allow for a half-grille, the use of two heavy wooden blocks, suspended approximately half a metre (19in) apart in the doorway, (see diagram) will effect a cure. They should be hung at around 1.7m (5ft 6in) from the ground to be effective on a horse 15 hands high. When he tries to weave they will bang his head. He will only do it a couple of times before he gives up. He can stand with his head over the door quite happily with them in place and still be able to see what is going on around him. It must be stressed that the wooden blocks used must be round and have no sharp corners or edges on which he could hurt himself. A pair of tie-logs from the saddlers might be suitable. Never use such items as house bricks, as they could do untold damage to the horse's face, particularly his eyes, before he finds out what is going to happen when he tries to weave and the bricks start swinging.

While it is not possible to actually cure a horse permanently of weaving, the above method of alleviating the problem will at least stop the damaging physical side-affects, which can be irreparable, assuming that he has not been weaving for any great length of time.

Rug-tearing

This is a most expensive bad habit which can be prevented quite easily.

There are two main causes. When young horses are first rugged up, their curiosity leads them to play with the rugs. As foals they will habitually grasp anything in their teeth, and the first signs of this habit must be checked immediately with a quick slap or a sharp word. All buckle tongues should be slipped home into their keepers when rugging-up is done. This immediately removes obvious projections which might be chewed and lead on to the habit.

The other main cause, more usual with adult horses, is overheating by having too much clothing on. It is important to regulate the number of rugs and blankets worn by the horse to coincide with temperature changes, especially in winter. The temperature at night may be considerably higher during a mild period and it is then necessary to take off that 'extra blanket' to avoid the horse becoming overheated.

In their natural environment, horses survive the winter outside with the coat that nature provides. The domesticated horse bred today may be clipped out for the colder months, but the temperature inside his stable may be 11°C (20°F) higher than outside. While it is obviously necessary to keep the horse sufficiently warm, the habit of trying to tear off rugs often starts where the horse is much too hot.

The first signs of such discomfort are that his rugs may slip badly in the night and his bedding may be very untidy. It is likely that the horse has rolled a lot in an attempt to rid himself of his clothing. Having dislodged them sufficiently, he may then tear them in trying to pull them off altogether. Either way, he will end up extremely uncomfortable.

An irritating side-effect is that, once this habit is established, it can lead to the offender tearing the rugs of his companions whilst out in the field. It is therefore very important not to allow it to develop, or it will be extremely costly and annoying.

It is relatively easy to prevent a horse from tearing at his clothing by attaching a bib to his headcollar, which he will be required to wear constantly. When correctly fitted this bib will stop the horse grasping his rugs with his teeth, as it will come between his teeth and his clothing. The lower edge of the bib must therefore extend approximately 5cm (2in) below the level of his lower lip. The bib can be made of any suitable strong material; leather is probably the best

A leather or strong material bib which is attached to the headcollar to prevent the horse eating his rugs. This may be bought or made specially by a saddler.

as it will not chafe the skin. It must be fairly stout leather, so it will not curl at the bottom edge, which would make it useless.

A proprietory brand paste such as 'Cribox' can be applied to New Zealand rugs worn by horses sharing a field with a horse who tears rugs. It is rather sticky, but well worth trying, as one application may be sufficient to discourage the habit. Applying 'Cribox' to the horse's own rugs in the first instance may prevent it becoming firmly established.

Bed-eating

Bed-eating is mainly prevalent amongst horses standing on straw. When eaten in large quantities, it can cause serious digestive and respiratory disorders and will affect the performance of horses doing fast or prolonged work, for example, the racehorse, eventer and hunter.

There are three types of straw which can be used for bedding: wheat, oat and barley straw. Wheat straw is generally the most sought-after. Good wheat straw should be of medium length, a good yellow colour and free from dust, mustiness and damp. Short straw makes a shallow bed and can be wasteful; although it is useful when bedding down a lame horse, as it will not be dragged about or constrict his movement. Long straw is easily moved around by the horse and can cause bare patches on the stable floor where he may damage his elbows or hocks if he lies down and rolls.

Barley straw is not very good bedding as a rule unless the crop was harvested well; the prickly beards can discourage a horse from lying down, especially if he is clipped out. If he never lies down he will probably not get sufficient rest. If the horse tries to eat barley straw, the beards may get lodged in the throat and cause choking. However, barley straw is usually of good quality and texture and makes a good clean bed.

Oat straw will almost certainly be eaten by most horses in some quantity and this straw is the most likely to trigger off habitual bed-eating. It is often fed as a substitute to horses who are allergic to hay and it is advantageous in the feeding of horses who have suffered from broken wind. Oat straw and hay together are often used as a good mixture to feed ponies wintering out when the cost of hay is prohibitive. When used for bedding, however, it can be too short, and is often non-elastic in texture, so is less popular than wheat or barley straw.

Horses start eating their bedding for a number of reasons. It may be that they are not receiving a sufficient ration of hay and so when they have finished it they begin picking through their bedding at night. It may be boredom, which is a very dangerous state for a horse to be in; or it may be a result of deprived appetite, caused by the horse lacking some essential element in his diet. If so he may not only be attracted to his bedding, but eat soiled bedding and even droppings, which will cause digestive disorders.

A precautionary worm dose and a quick revision of your horse's diet sheet may put things right. Regular or at least occasional addition of cod liver oil, linseed and a vitamin and mineral additive is necessary and definitely a regular intake of sufficient salt. To ensure that the horse receives enough salt in his diet, install a salt lick holder in his stable, in which you can put ordinary rock salt or a mineral salt lick, either of which should be available from a corn merchant.

When brought into a clean stable with a fresh bed most horses will immediately start to pick through their straw, searching for soft grasses which are usually in it; if it is observed that the horse is eating large quantities of bedding, which will be apparent from the lack of straw left by morning, it will be necessary to try to prevent him.

All bedding should be very carefully mucked out daily as a matter of course; and regular skipping out throughout the day, if the horse lives in, will ensure that the bed remains as clean as possible. It is easy to make the straw smell distasteful to the horse by mixing some strong-smelling but mild disinfectant with water and sprinkling the solution over the bedding with a watering-can, being very careful not to make the straw wet. This will usually discourage him from eating it.

Alternatively, you can try a different sort of bedding, probably the best being wood shavings. These make an extremely good bed that is easy to manage, are light, dry and relatively dust-free if good quality, and easy to muck out. They are also ideal for deep-litter, or semi-deep-litter, which in this day and age appears sound economy. The soiled areas are easy to find and the floor will not become too wet nor the box smelly as a result of the horse staling, as the shavings quickly absorb the fluid before it spreads. Even in a deep-litter box, the ammonia fumes rise less from shavings than from straw and therefore the stables remain sweet-smelling, obviously an advantage for the horse's respiratory system. The one drawback is that it is not always easy to dispose of the manure.

Sawdust however, is not recommended as it is very dusty, and usually difficult to dispose of. It will quickly ball up inside and 'draw' the horse's feet. In time, this can cause the sole to become soft and thin and render the horse more likely to go lame on rough going. If sawdust is to be used, it is therefore necessary to pick out his feet regularly and often.

Peat is a fairly difficult bedding to manage well, as it is heavy when wet, and being dark in colour, it is difficult to find the soiled patches and wet areas. The disposal of peat manure can also present a problem.

Should the horse attempt to eat any of the alternative types of bedding, sprinkling a solution of mild disinfectant over it, as described, should soon stop him.

3 Running back, escaping and barging

Running back or pulling back

This is one of the most dangerous habits that a horse can pick up, as it usually results in him getting loose and unless he is in an enclosed yard, he is likely to get out on to the road. Horses are not used to complete freedom, being always restricted in some way, and this new-found liberty often leads to panic, resulting in disaster. Less serious is that it can be very expensive to replace broken headcollars, if leather ones are used.

This 'trick', as it can become, is usually learned in one of the following ways. Fear is the most common cause in the first instance, as flight is the horse's natural instinctive reaction to any danger. For example – a horse who is tied up in the yard and startled by a tractor suddenly coming around the corner will instinctively jump and may try to break loose by running back. Having done so, he is then free to run away, and likely also to panic, having been frightened. Youngsters are particularly susceptible as they do not have enough experience of life to know that such things as tractors may be safely ignored. It is a mistake to leave a young horse tied up outside unattended.

Teaching a young horse to stand quietly when tied up is an essential part of his basic training, and sufficient thought and time must be devoted to doing it properly. This training should be done in the stable to begin with – never outside.

In the early stages, he should never be left on his own. Start by tying him up for his grooming or when he is given his feed. In this way, his mind will be partially occupied by something pleasant. (As a rule, all horses enjoy being groomed, unless it is done carelessly). The period of time for which he may be tied up will depend on the individual horse and should be increased very gradually. The first time the horse is left tied up alone should not be for longer than a minute or so, and it is a good idea for his trainer to hide somewhere where he can observe his horse's reactions, without being seen by the horse – e.g., in the box next door, if it has a knot in the woodwork through which to look. If he stands patiently, do not be tempted to leave him too long, or he will lose his patience and start digging up the bedding or chewing on the headcollar rope. If he starts digging the moment you leave him or swings back and forth calling out, then talk to him; this may soothe him even though he cannot see you. When you return to the box, make much of him, even if he has not been 'the model child'; and never reprimand him in these early stages. To shout at him or strike him at all would probably make him pull back on the rope – the one thing you want to avoid at this stage.

It is very important that the headcollar rope should not be directly tied to the tie-ring; for should the horse panic when you leave the box, and slip and fall, he will be hung up and could hurt himself badly if the headcollar does not break. A piece of binder twine in a loop, attached to the tie-ring, will give quite easily under such circumstances, but unless old and worn, will not give way if the horse merely pulls back. This should be replaced from time to time.

When tying up use a quick release knot. The binder twine is a safety precaution -- a 'weak link' that will break in case of emergency.

The second cause of running back is tying horses up by their reins, an unforgivable thing to do, which can lead directly to fear of being tied up. If the horse is startled and jumps about when tied up by his bridle, he will hurt his mouth. Also, bridles break very easily, being made of narrow leather.

A third and common cause of this habit is tying horses up with too long a rope – often done when they are left tied up to eat feeds from a bucket on the ground. First they put a foot over the rope, then when they try to raise their heads, they discover that the rope is caught around a leg, and all but an old, wise and sensible horse will panic and break loose.

Lastly – horseboxes and trailers are renowned for causing problems of all kinds and this is one. When their surroundings become unfamiliar horses are more inclined to unusual behaviour because their instincts take over. Not all horses travel regularly, and not all horse owners have their own transport. Therefore, the majority of horses who travel often find themselves in totally unknown surroundings, so will have all their wits about them, and may, quite reasonably, be on edge.

Having led the horse up into the trailer or box, he should not be tied up until he is secured into his compartment, i.e., by the partition in a box, or the breeching strap in a trailer. Should anything happen to startle him before he is secured when he is already tied up, he will be very likely to try and get out of the box. A horse trying to escape from a box at high speed when frightened usually ends up 'in tears'. This situation can easily be prevented by a little forethought.

Once the habit of pulling back has been established and is used as a 'trick', there is not much than can be done to cure it. It is a great nuisance not to be able to tie up your horse whenever and wherever you want to – for example, when you go to a show and you find that you must spend all day loading and unloading your horse into the box instead of tying him up to it as the classes come and go; which might not even be so easy if he does not load very well! The value of preventing him from learning this habit is sometimes not fully apppreciated until the habit is established. Prevention, in this case, is the very best cure.

The important rules to remember when tying up your horse are as follows:-

1 Never leave young horses tied up outside unattended.
2 Never leave horses tied up unattended on a long rope, i.e., at feeding time.
3 Never tie a horse up by his bridle.
4 Never tie a horse up in unfamiliar surroundings unless you are sure that he is sensible and has settled properly.
5 Never tie a horse up to wire fencing, cars, lorries, etc., or anything on which he might hurt himself.
6 Never tie a horse up too close to another – he might be kicked or threatened by the other horse and try to get away.

If the habit shows itself in a young horse as the result of him being startled, then in time, with careful handling, and good management, it may be erased. Reassurance, soothing words and patience can all go a long way to help the nervous youngster gain confidence in his surroundings. The sense never to put him in a position whereby he can be frightened into pulling back will nearly always be rewarded.

However, horses who pull back purely as a trick to get free have to be prevented from doing it. It may be possible to cure them. Firstly, when they are brought into the yard, it is easier to put them in a stable instead of tying them up and agitating the problem, although this may not always be possible.

The use of hobbles will prevent a horse from running anywhere, including running back, but they can be dangerous until he gets used to them, as, they may make him fall to begin with. For the first few occasions hobbles should be fitted inside a stable which is well bedded down, with the horse wearing kneecaps in case of accident. Never attempt to fit them for the first time with the horse standing on concrete or any hard surface. If necessary, seek expert help until you know how to use them properly.

It may be possible to re-train the horse who pulls back by the following method, but it must be supervised carefully, and requires a certain amount of expertise to be carried out correctly and safely.

The method consists of tying the horse up by his headcollar rope in the normal way, i.e., to the tie-ring via a piece of twine, and fitting a secondary set of thick cotton ropes on to him.

It is very important that the lower of the two ropes, which acts as a breeching strap, must be shorter than the headcollar rope. This will ensure that the horse is pressured from behind the quarters as he steps back, before he actually starts to pull on the headcollar rope to

twine securely tied
to strong rings

thick soft cotton ropes

ropes tied to twine loops with quick-release knots

Fitting cotton ropes on to a horse who pulls back. The rope from the horse's body
must be tied to a very secure fitting.

break free. Obviously the ropes must be fairly stout to be effective;
but tie a short length of twine to the end of the rope and tie the twine
to the ring, so that the horse will be freed by the twine breaking in
case of emergency. Also, the knots used to tie him up should both be
quick-release knots.

As previously stated, this procedure must be supervised, and the
horse watched carefully from nearby. A lot of horses will not attempt
to run back when there is someone in sight and so it is probably best
to watch him from a hiding place. It must be done on a soft surface in
case of accident, and the ideal place is a well bedded-down loose box

with the door left wide open. If the door is shut, the horse is less likely to try and run back, but if it is open, and he is a real 'trickster', it will literally be an 'open invitation'.

Under these circumstances, it will probably not be long before the horse attempts to run back. When he does, you will find out whether or not you have set up the ropes correctly. Remember that cotton rope stretches to a certain extent, and that you are trying to avoid the horse getting loose by breaking his headcollar, so there must be quite a bit more slack on the headcollar rope than on the body ropes.

If the horse will not attempt to run back whilst in a stable, you may try this method out in a small paddock, but only if the ground is smooth and free from sharp stones. Be absolutely sure that the fence post you choose to tie him to is very strong and cannot be pulled out of the ground.

Escaping
Untying ropes
Some more intelligent horses and ponies develop the knack of untying ropes and opening door bolts, which is not only a nuisance, but can have damaging effects on them. Happily both these problems are relatively easy to prevent. If your horse unties ropes,

Fixing a second tie-ring to the stable wall and tying the horse up to both will prevent him untying the knots on either side.

pillar reins (two headcollar ropes) tied the same length

the substitution of a rack chain instead of a headcollar rope will be an effective preventative measure. An alternative is to fix another tie-ring to the stable wall, approximately 1.2m (4ft) away from the first, and pillar rein him, i.e., tie him up from both sides, so each rope prevents him reaching the knots of the other. (*See* diagram page 29).

Undoing bolts
Where butterfly bolts are fitted to the stables, a headcollar rope clip may be used to prevent the horse from undoing them with his teeth. Attach the clip to the bottom ring of the butterfly when the bolt is closed and the head pushed downwards. A butterfly bolt is usually the standard type of stable bolt used (*see* opposite, above right). This type of lock is designed for use with a padlock, but it is vital that a horse is never locked into his stable, because in the event of fire or other emergency, it would take longer to get him out; and even more serious, no one without a key would be able to free him in his owner's absence.

You can also buy an ordinary type butterfly bolt which has a spring attachment and can be opened with one hand, but cannot be opened at all by a horse.

You may be able to purchase a purpose-made stable door bolt, which, once properly shut, requires both hands to open it, one hand lifting a hidden plate inside the bolt from underneath, which will release the opening mechanism (*see* opposite, below right).

Whichever type of bolt you have at the top of the stable door, be sure to fit a bottom bolt too and keep it shut at all times. If the bottom bolt is to be an ordinary door bolt, a lot of extra time will be spent in bending up and down. It would be much better to fit one known as a 'kick bolt' (*see* opposite, left). This should be fitted at a height of approximately 30cm (1ft) from the ground. It consists of a metal plate on a swivel, with two catches for it to rest on, one of which is attached to the door and the other to the door post. At one end of the swivel plate the metal is moulded around to give a protruding lip for the foot to strike to open and close it. The kick bolt is available from saddlers and farm equipment stores.

Barging
Horses who escape by barging past you when you open the door can also be quite easily stopped. Attach a removable bar across the

Butterfly stable bolt.

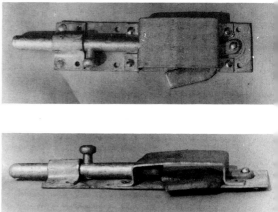

Above Kick bolt in open position.

Top Kick bolt in closed position. This is used on the bottom of the stable door.

Above Purpose-made stable bolt viewed from below.

Top Purpose-made stable bolt.

31

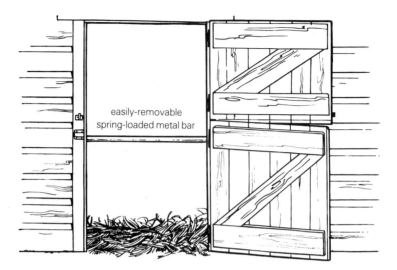

easily-removable
spring-loaded metal bar

An anti-barging bar. A slip rail is also suitable. It can be fixed in any way inside the stable which enables the door to be opened. It must be fitted so that it can be lifted out quickly.

doorway, from one door post to the other on the inside of the stable. (*See* above). Fit it on a level with the horse's chest; however, do remember that is there yourself until you both get used to it!

Horses who barge as a general rule, in field gateways and such places, have probably not been brought up properly as youngsters, having been allowed to do as they pleased without correction. They are fairly easy to re-school in their manners, and the fault of barging must be dealt with straightaway, each time it appears. Quite often, a sharp slap across the snout will have the desired effect. It may also be necessary to carry a stick when you go to the field in order to avoid being stepped or trampled on in the gateway by the barging horse. This is especially so at haying-up time, for example, when the horses will probably be crowded around the gate and good manners are sometimes forgotten.

Some horses attempt to barge away when being led past the hay barn or feed room. This type of barging is less likely to result in the leader of the horse being hurt, but it is nonetheless necessary to stop the habit. It is most commonly found in childrens' ponies, as children are not always capable of controlling them, due to lack of strength and size. Such ponies do not have the same degree of success when trying to barge with an adult, and in fact may not even attempt to barge off when being led by an older person, being crafty enough to know they will not get away with it so easily.

When a horse or pony is wearing only a headcollar the amount of control possible is limited, so putting on a bridle will help. It is wise for the person leading to wear gloves, to prevent the reins from slipping through the fingers, which can cause nasty burns to the hands. Woollen gloves are not very effective as they will not prevent slipping – leather gloves are best. It must be stressed that on no account must the horse or pony be jabbed in the mouth if he attempts to barge off. This may result in a bad mouth sore, and can also cause the animal to become headshy or bridle-shy.

A stick may be carried to remind the horse of his manners, but must only ever be applied to the shoulder. However, when the horse is wearing a bridle and his handler wearing gloves, hopefully all the extra help required will be a sharp word of reinforcement of the handler's wishes.

A useful tip is to tie a knot in the end of your horse's headcollar rope, (opposite end to the headcollar clip). This will prevent the rope from slipping right through your hands and the horse getting away from you when wearing only his headcollar. It is a good rule of thumb to adopt, when handling youngstock in particular, as they are more likely to pull away if frightened and must not be allowed to get loose. A horse who discovers that he can get free from his handler by pulling away is only one stop away from learning the art of 'running back' when tied up. (*See* Running back page 24).

4 Grooming, pulling and clipping difficulties

Grooming

Grooming is part of a horse's daily routine and most horses enjoy it thoroughly if it is done properly. It should be a time the horse looks forward to, not something that he has to 'put up with'. Each horse must be catered for differently, according to his needs. It is important to understand fully which pieces of grooming kit should be used for which purpose; incorrect use of grooming tools can cause unintentional suffering to the horse. If he is not to be allowed to enjoy being groomed, it will not be long before he is seen swishing his tail and laying back his ears – the first signs of kicking and biting. (*see* Chapter 7).

How a horse should be groomed depends upon whether he is clipped and living in or hairy and living out, and this will also dictate the amount of grooming he will need. Nature teaches horses and ponies to roll in the mud in winter, because it soon dries on them and gives an extra protective layer against the wind. However, when they are brought in to be ridden, the mud will have to be cleaned off. The dandy brush is designed for this, and it is fairly efficient on dry mud, but wet mud and clay will clog it up in no time, so it may not always be efficient. While it is unforgivable to use a metal curry comb for wet mud, a plastic curry comb used with care is very effective and can be washed regularly. When they are damp from the winter air, manes and tails can be difficult to deal with. The hairs become stretchy when damp, and if they are tangled and muddy, care must be taken not to damage them. Tails should be brushed from the bottom upwards to avoid pulling out the long hairs, and again the plastic curry comb is ideal for this. The tail should be held in one hand while combed with the other, to prevent the hair from being pulled out by the roots; regular attention will stop bad tangles from forming. Manes, in particular, should not be washed regularly in the winter, as

34

it is almost impossible to dry the horse properly when he has a thick winter coat. If the tail is washed, take care not to wet the legs, especially the heels, as these may become cracked and sore from oil being removed from the skin by shampoo. Wet muddy legs should not be brushed; this may cause mud fever, which is brought about by being brushed into the open pores of the skin. The body brush should not be used on the coat of horses who live out, as it removes too much of the natural oil which nature provides as waterproofing. The dandy brush should be used on the coat once the worst of the mud has been removed.

The stable-kept horse who is clipped out needs completely different care. The dandy brush should only be used on the legs if they are not clipped, and then only when the legs are completely dry. A dandy brush must never be used on the body as it is much too hard. The body brush is designed for this purpose and should be used on the mane and tail also. These should be brushed out daily so they do not develop tangles. Keeping the tail tidy by regular brushing will also reduce the number of hairs which will fall out. It is very easy to ruin a tail if care is not taken; the long hairs are pulled out faster than the horse can grow them!

Brush tails as you would brush your own long hair – gently and starting from the bottom, working upwards carefully freeing any tangles.

A stable rubber or a wisp should be used to strap the muscles of the neck and quarters which will help to get and keep the horse fit; this will also tone up his circulation and keep him warm.

It is important not to let the clipped horse get cold while he is being groomed, so his rugs should be folded back over the loins when grooming the forehand and then folded up over the shoulders when the hindquarters are done. He should never be left standing without his rugs on at grooming time or he will get chilly and miserable.

All horses should have their feet picked out regularly and have their eyes, noses and docks cleaned. Two sponges should be used – one for the eyes and nose and the other for the dock. With a gelding, the sheath must also be kept clean and the mare should have her udder checked regularly. This is especially important in winter when the sheath or udder can get very dirty from mud flying up and will become sore if not attended to properly. Great care must be taken when dealing with both areas as they are very delicate and highly sensitive; if not handled very gently the horse will undoubtedly lodge an objection. They should be bathed with a sponge, cotton wool or an old flannel and warm water but never soap, as it is an irritant.

Whichever category your horse is in, one of these methods of grooming should cater for his needs. If done as described, carefully, the horse should have no cause for complaint. However, there are horses who are difficult to groom and can react violently to it; it is important to understand why before you can begin to do anything about it.

If previous rough handling and misuse of the grooming kit is the reason, then a little time and patience and the use of correct methods will see an improvement in behaviour.

The most common causes for bad behaviour however, are found with Thoroughbreds, who are frequently thin-skinned and very ticklish. The most sensitive areas of the horse are usually the stifle region, the girth area behind the elbows and often the belly and flanks. Special consideration must be taken to see that these horses do not truly 'suffer' during their grooming.

To begin with, the choice of grooming tools must be reconsidered. Body brushes are made either from nylon fibres or real bristles; nylon ones are much harder. Bristle brushes, although soft, do just as good a job. They cost more, but the horse will certainly appreciate the extra expense. There are however a few horses that are too thin-skinned and ticklish to be brushed at all, and a folded stable rubber is all that can be used. This can be slightly damped to increase its efficiency, but it must be followed by the use of a dry rubber for strapping to ensure that the horse is not left damp or he may catch a chill.

Horses should always be tied up to be groomed and should obviously behave themselves properly. If your horse tries to bite you, tie him up sufficiently short to prevent it, or in the extreme, fit a muzzle while you groom him, for your own protection. It is a mistake to stand too far away from a horse who is likely to kick out when you are working around his hindquarters. The closer you keep to him the less likely he is to be able to kick you and he will not be able to kick nearly as hard if you are right next to him. If he does lash out, then obviously he must be reprimanded. A sharp word and a slap should suffice, but this must be followed by reassurance and soft words. Remember that while you must have discipline, grooming must not become a running battle between you both; so although you must command respect, this should be tempered with a great deal of sympathy in your actions, and kindness in attitude. (*See* Chapter 7).

Horses should never be disturbed when they are eating, so grooming should not be done then. It is a natural instinct for a horse to protect himself when he is feeding and he may well warn off intruders; attempting to groom at this time is asking for trouble. However, it may be advantageous to allow him a haynet while being groomed, to give him something to keep his mind on. This should not have the same effect as giving hard feed; for the horse who habitually stands on three legs, digging madly when he has a corn feed, will rarely attack a haynet with the same enthusiasm, so his instinctive protective attitude will also be diminished.

Mane and tail pulling
Pulling manes and tails is an acquired art, but is easy once you have the knack of knowing which hairs to pull out. It must be done gradually and carefully, so the horse does not suffer, particularly with the tail; this involves pullings hairs out by the roots which may cause bleeding. Manes and tails should be pulled regularly, i.e., little and often. If you need to plait your horse regularly, such as for hunting or showing, it will be easier to plait if the mane is short and even.

If a horse or pony has a long shaggy mane or tail, you cannot expect to pull it all at once; it must be done over a period of several weeks. Attempting to pull it all at once is usually the initial reason for horses misbehaving on subsequent occasions, as they will be hurt and will remember it.

When a horse is unfit and in soft condition, his hair may be pulled out far more readily than when he is fit and hard, so hunters coming up from grass in preparation for the new season should have their manes and tails done before they start to get fit. It is also much easier to pull the hairs out when the horse is warm, i.e., after exercise, when the pores are still open, than when he is 'cold' – before work.

Although a horse is never likely to enjoy having his mane or tail pulled, it must be made as pleasant for him as possible; and his co-operation will be needed if it is to be done at all. Some horses persist in shaking their heads when the mane is being done – others

Buy a narrow mane comb like the one above. It is much easier to use than a wider one when you want to pull a mane very short.

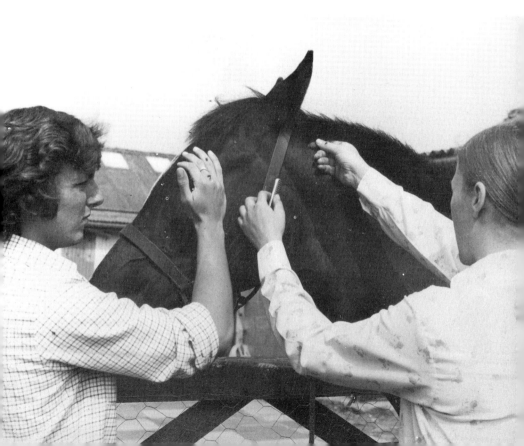

Straw bales used to prevent a horse striking out while the mane is being pulled. This horse's mane grows naturally on the near-side and I will correct this over a period of time by pulling it on the off-side and plaiting it over afterwards.

may develop the knack of tossing their heads just as you reach for a piece of hair. Either way, it is easier to have an assistant on hand to hold the horse's head steady, and it will be a help if he covers the horse's eye with one hand so that he cannot see you reaching up to his mane. It may also be advantageous for you to stand on an upturned feed tin so that you can reach easily, especially if the horse is very tall. If the horse swings round and tries to squash you against the wall, or attempts to strike out with a foreleg, use a couple of straw bales on top of one another, or, ideally, a partition between stalls.

The trailer, although it may be ideal for such restraint, should not be used if there is any choice. It may cause the horse to become bad at loading, by associating the trailer with mane-pulling, if it is something to which he violently objects. Using a twitch (*see* page 48) however, may often provide an instant solution to your problems.

39

The mane

Always pull the hairs out from the underside of the mane, never from the top. If these are removed, they will not only stick upright when they are growing back, but will be impossible to plait in. After you have pulled the mane, it may be necessary to damp it and plait it up for twenty-four hours to make it stay on the correct (off) side.

Never be tempted to cut the mane with scissors. The result will look terrible, and because the mane will not have been suitably thinned out, it will probably stand up on end like the mane of a zebra within a day or so. By cutting it short, you will have taken the weight out of it, which previously kept it lying down. Having cut it, you may be tempted to hog the mane. Hogging is not a good idea unless your horse has a very wide crest and a growth of hair that is really unmanageable. The mane is nature's protection from the wind and flies. While hogging manes saves plaiting regularly, in the case of hunters etc., and is often done for this reason, the horse will have no defence from flies around his head in the summer, or the wind in winter when he is turned out. This is one reason why the docking of tails was made illegal. Another thing to consider if you intend to hog the mane is whether the horse has a good enough neck to carry it off – a poor neck will look even worse if the mane is hogged.

The tail

Tails can be more difficult to pull than manes, as the dock is very sensitive. While the hairs are often easier to pull out of the tail than the mane, bleeding is more likely to occur from the tail. Horses soon learn to swing their quarters from side to side to resist having their tails pulled and indeed may try to kick out if they find it uncomfortable. As you will be standing directly behind the horse, you will be directly in the line of fire. Again, you can use a couple of straw bales on top of one another, and put the horse to stand in a stall rather than a loose box, to help keep him straight. In this case also, the trailer should be avoided if possible for the reasons mentioned above; but if all else fails, it may be the only answer. If you have an assistant who can hold the horse steady for you (again, the twitch may come in handy), you may be able to pull the tail efficiently from over the stable door. As it will not be important to keep the horse's head still to do the tail, your assistant can try to persuade the horse to co-operate by holding a bucket with some nuts in it for him. If this works, then it is obviously preferable to resorting to the twitch.

Carry a dressage whip when teaching your horse to lead properly, so that you can touch him on the flank with it and send him forward.

The correct way to lead on the road, that is, facing oncoming traffic, with the horse on the kerbside.

When the foal is very small, use only one rope to lead him thus. Note that a knot at the end of the rope is a good deterrent against losing hold when there is a battle, even with a grown horse.

The rope around the quarters creates pressure forwards.

Wear an over-jacket to warn motorists to give you a wide berth. Different ones are available, some with wording such as: CAUTION – YOUNG HORSE.

Only pull out a couple of hairs at a time, and always use your fingers, not a comb, when pulling tails. On a tail which has been pulled regularly in the past, the hairs will probably be too short to use a comb. When dealing with a tail that has not been pulled previously, using a comb will encourage pulling out too many hairs at a time from one place. Only pull hairs from the underside of the tail – never the top, otherwise bald patches will result, eventually followed by short stubby patches of hair which will stick out and look terrible. If the tail is bandaged at night, the long top hairs will soon set tidily in place.

As a last resort, you may find that tranquillizing is helpful. However, unlike clipping which may only need doing twice or three times a year, tails need to be kept pulled approximately once a month so it will be expensive in vet's bills. It may not necessarily be successful; the horse will still be able to feel what is happening to him and may harm himself if he tries to resist. His reactions will be dulled and his balance impeded by the tranquillizer, which could make him fall down if he struggles excessively.

In some cases, tail-pulling will not be possible; if not, for a horse who lives in at night, bandaging the tail will set it fair and keep it tidy. A tail should not be damped too much before being bandaged, as this will cause the bandage to tighten as it dries out from the heat of the horse's skin, and this shrinkage will cause considerable discomfort. Old and inelastic bandages should not be used either as they can easily slip off or be rubbed off and will be lost or soiled in the horse's bed.

If your horse really will not stand (literally) to have his tail pulled, then grow it out and plait it when you want to show or hunt, and keep it bandaged at night if he lives in. Plaiting the tail is time-consuming and will mean getting up even earlier in the mornings, but the result is very attractive and worth the extra effort. Most judges like to see a plaited tail and in classes where turnout is important, it may well be a point in your favour.

Clipping

Clipping a horse can be easy, or it can be almost impossible. A number of otherwise benign horses become unrecognizable when the clippers are switched on. Clipping is almost a necessity for most horses who are in work during the winter months, as it is impossible to clean and dry them properly when their coats are caked with mud

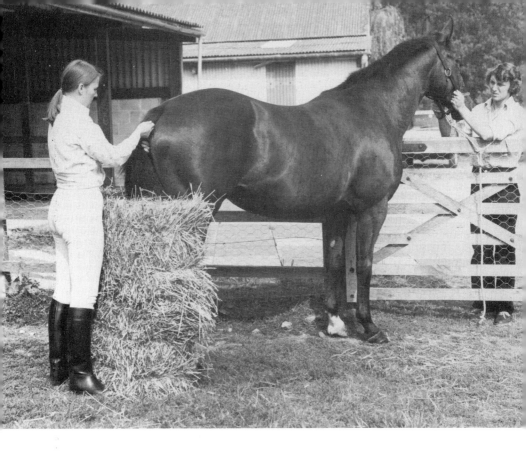

Again, when tail pulling, use straw bales as a barricade to avoid receiving a nasty kick. Place them as close to the horse as possible and stand right up against them yourself.

and sweat, for example, after a day's hunting. Leaving mud and sweat on the coat can easily lead to coughs and colds, chills or even pneumonia. Only do clipping yourself if you are competent.

The most common cause for fear of the clippers must be previous bad experiences. Horses are highly sensitive to noise, and clippers are very noisy, but most of them soon get used to this and it ceases to be a problem. Several things can cause fear; highest on the list are cuts and burns. Areas of the body such as the stifle and elbow are very sensitive in any case, and are particularly difficult to clip as they have folds of loose, soft skin. It is very easy to accidently chop into these areas if great care is not taken. Burning by overheated clippers can easily be avoided and is therefore unforgivable. This is caused by the blades becoming clogged up with hair or not being sharp enough; and when they are tightened up, this makes the motor work harder and so the clippers overheat. The quickest way to blunt the blades is to try to clip a dirty horse. The blades end up trying to chew their way through the hair instead of cutting cleanly, obviously most unpleasant for the horse. Regular cleaning and oiling of the clippers during use should stop them from getting too hot. If they do overheat, stop clipping at once until they have cooled down again. It is a good idea to have a least one spare pair of blades at the ready, in case of breakage or blunting, as once you have started to clip your horse, you will want to finish the job.

To begin with, consider a young horse being clipped for the first time. It is important to remember that this first experience with clippers will be indelibly printed on his mind for the rest of his life, and you cannot therefore be too careful and patient. Never attempt to clip any horse unless you have sufficient time to do it properly. You must be in a position to give the young horse all the time he needs to adjust to these new proceedings.

You will need a stable with plenty of light so that you can see what you are doing, and an assistant to help to keep the horse calm. He should have first been thoroughly groomed for the reasons above, and his tail bandaged up and out of harm's way. (The mane and forelock should be bunched up into rubber bands when attempting a full clip so they are not damaged; however, it will not be necessary in this instance.)

The first thing that will probably happen when you switch on the clippers initially is that the youngster will jump out of his skin, stare at the clippers and snort. This is quite natural and he should be allowed to inspect them when they have been switched off again. While they are still switched off, they should be run over the horse's coat in a gentle stroking motion, and at the same time, the horse should be soothed and petted. When he begins to relax, take them away from his skin and switch them on again. He will probably react in much the same way and he should be reassured again. Switch them off and run them lightly over him once more and when this procedure has been repeated several times, he should begin to relax. Eventually, you should be able to put them against his coat while they are switched on without him minding; the best place to start is the shoulder area. It is a good idea for the assistant to have some pony cubes in a bucket to use for rewarding and keeping the horse happy. If he trusts you, which will depend on the previous relationship you have shared with him, he should have confidence in you whatever you do to him, so clipping should not present much of a problem once the initial stages are over. However, to attempt more than clipping-out his neck, chest and belly on the first occasion is asking too much. Doing these areas alone will take up the maximum amount of time you should ask the young horse to stand quietly for the first occasion.

If all has gone well, the next attempt may be a trace clip, but clipping the head is not recommended until the youngster is quite confident. If he were to put up a fight, he would win by reason of his superior strength, and someone could easily be hurt. To use a twitch to restrain him when fear is the cause of his resistance would be unforgivable and probably make him difficult to clip for the rest of his life.

Ticklish, thin-skinned horses will rarely be easy to clip and they must be handled with great patience if they are to be clipped at all. It is possible to have your veterinary surgeon tranquillize a horse for clipping, but this is not always successful, as it is difficult to judge a sufficient dose, and the effects may begin to wear off before you have finished. However, it may be the only way with certain horses and although it is quite expensive, you may be able to get away with as little as two clips during the winter. The advantages of clipping, if it is possible, far outweigh the disadvantages.

Using a twitch

If you own a horse who is awkward to clip because he is merely misbehaving and you know he is not in the least frightened and is old and wise enough to know better, you may find that putting a twitch on him may restore his good manners and make him stand still, which is important for his own safety. However, if he is in any way frightened, the use of a twitch is out of the question. A twitch must always be put on the horse's top lip – never anywhere else.

You can make your own twitch, rather than buying one, by cutting approximately 45cm (18in) off the end of an old broom handle and drilling a hole through it about 2.5cm (1in) from the end. Pass a piece of binder twine about 25cm (10in) long through the hole and knot the ends securely, then push the knot inside the hole, out of sight. Both ends of the handle should be smoothed and rounded

You must be experienced to use a twitch and you need at least one assistant, preferably two. This is a homemade twitch held properly in both hands. If two assistants are not available, the horse must be tied up short so that he cannot rear up and pull the twitch free from the handler.

where they have been sawn off, especially the end that has the twitch string through it. A leather bootlace may be used instead of twine.

The twitch must always be held in place by an assistant, who must use both hands to hold on to it. If the horse tosses his head and the assistant accidently lets go of it, the horse could badly damage his head, especially his eyes as he will shake his head about violently until the twitch falls off. The assistant who was holding the twitch could be hurt also.

Do not twist the twitch tighter than absolutely necessary and never leave it on for too long at any one time. If you need to use it for any length of time, take it off and clip some other part of the horse. When you remove it, always give the horse's lip a good rub, to help restore circulation.

Only use a twitch if you are experienced.

5 Problems when preparing to ride

Catching your horse

If a horse is difficult to catch, the most obvious reason is probably that he does not enjoy what is going to happen to him once he has been caught. An unfit or overweight horse or pony subjected to hard work by an overzealous rider is obviously not going to enjoy being ridden and will avoid being caught if he can. A large number of horses and ponies suffer from inactivity from Monday to Friday and from overwork at weekends and during holidays. It is difficult to keep them fit when they can only be exercised at weekends and therefore the amount and content of work must be carefully scheduled so as not to cause overworking.

If back sores, bit sores or girth galls occur the animal is probably suffering from soft condition coupled with too much work. It may also be that his tack is not correctly fitted, another important factor which is easily remedied to avoid unnecessary discomfort. No horse or pony will enjoy his work if he is unfit and tired or his tack is uncomfortable. Good management and a watchful eye will help to ensure that he does not become bad to catch.

When they are difficult to catch horses must never be chased or shouted at; and to punish them when they allow themselves to be caught 'at last' is unkind and stupid and will only compound the problem for future occasions. If you are in danger of losing your temper because you are trailing after your horse yet again – and it can be exceedingly frustrating – then the best thing is to leave him alone, rather than risk 'taking it out on him' when he would not understand why he was being punished.

However, let us assume that you have bought a horse that you cannot catch. You will want to set about curing him straightaway and although this is relatively easy on the whole, you will need a great deal of time and patience. If the necessary amenities are not available, you will have to be imaginative and improvise.

You will need a field or small paddock where your horse can be turned out on his own. Ideally it should be one without too much keep so that he will retain his appetite. If he is wearing a headcollar it will be easier to catch him when the times comes, but it is very important that it fits him properly. A headcollar which is too tight will not allow him to graze properly and could rub badly. One which is too big may easily be lost when he rubs on a tree or fence post, but the worst danger is that he might catch a hind foot in it whilst trying to scratch himself and could be severely hurt in attempting to get free. Never be tempted to leave even a short length of rope attached to a headcollar when your horse is turned out wearing it, as horses move along as they graze, placing their front feet very close to their heads, and it will not be many minutes before your horse steps on the rope. The moment he tries to raise his head, he will break the headcollar if it is leather, or if it is nylon and will not break, he will suffer repeated blows on the poll from treading on the rope repeatedly.

First you must teach your horse to associate your coming to the field with pleasant thoughts, and the more often you can visit him the better – ideally two or three times each day. Take something nice for him to eat – a few pieces of carrot or apple, or pony nuts, but do not make any attempt to catch him to begin with. Talk to him in a soft, low, reassuring voice and get as close to him as you can without him moving away. Try to coax him to come to you, but do not be disappointed if you get nowhere to begin with. Take the nuts or titbits and put them in a feed tin or other suitable container. If you cannot persuade your horse to come and eat out of it, leave it in the field with him. After you have gone, you can bet that he will investigate it and find a nice surprise. When you come back later, repeat the process. After a few visits, your horse will begin to associate your coming with something nice and the fact that you have not actually tried to catch him will begin to create trust in his mind.

It is hoped that your horse will soon gain the confidence at least to begin to come towards you. The next step is to try to coax him to eat out of the bowl while you are holding it, if gingerly at first. When he is quite happy about doing this, try putting one hand in the bowl with the food and let him touch you with his muzzle. Do not attempt to stroke him until he is confident about the closeness of your hand to his face. The great thing to remember is to be endlessly patient.

Watch him like a hawk, talk to him quietly and be sure that he is really ready before you try to touch him. When you do, he may run away immediately. Whatever you do, do not make a grab at him. At this stage, if he tries to take off and you hang on for grim death and get dragged halfway across the field on the end of the headcollar, all will be lost. Your horse will know he has been tricked and you could be back to square one. As soon as you feel that he is going to run away, just talk quietly to him, making no further attempt to touch him. Try to get him to eat from the bowl again and reassure him. Ignore the fact that he knows that you want to catch him and carry on as before. He is just not ready to give in completely and you have not gained enough of his confidence. In time, if you are patient, you will, literally, have him 'eating out of your hand'.

When he lets you take hold of the headcollar, clip your rope on to it, make a fuss of him and then let him go again. If you really want to re-train him to be good to catch, you must resist the temptation to rush him to the stable, tack-up and ride him. Wait until he is really good to catch. You will know when that is.

The cure is obviously only possible where you have a field or paddock for your sole use. It is not going to work in a field full of horses and ponies. Under those circumstances, all that will happen is that you will be surrounded by the other horses, long before you get near your horse. You may easily get kicked if you are carrying a bowl of food and several horses crowd around you.

The other reason why this method will not work when your horse is turned out with others is that horses are gregarious so are content to stay where there is company. They do not, as a rule, enjoy being on their own. When your horse is alone in his paddock, you will be his only company and his attention will be on you. Eventually, he will look forward to your coming, especially as you always bring him something nice to eat.

When you can successfully catch your horse whenever you want to, you face the problem of catching him when he is out with other horses. The system may break down as soon as you turn him out in company again, so if possible, turn one other horse out with him first in his paddock. I need hardly add that the new companion must be one who is very easy to catch, as his example to your own horse will be an obvious advantage. Assuming that all goes well, you can re-introduce your horse to his own field very soon with no further problems. However, if he is going to live in a very large field with good keep, you run the risk of the habit re-asserting itself. Ideally, he should be kept in a field where supplementary feeding is necessary so that his desire to be caught and fed will stay with him until he is firmly established as 'good to catch'.

This basic routine of catching and feeding is easily instilled into youngstock as a matter of course. It is also very easy to teach your horse to come to call by this method, a routine which is not only most rewarding, but has endless practical advantages.

Tacking-up

Many people who own and handle horses appear never to have had instruction in the 'art' of tacking-up correctly. It is a grave omission, because it is a procedure that must be done very carefully if it is not to cause the horse discomfort and create difficulty.

First consider how many things could cause the horse discomfort. From the bridle, he runs the risk of having his teeth bashed, his lips pinched, his eyes banged and his ears pinched and pulled around; from the saddle, his back can be chilled (if he is clipped and the lining is cold) and the folds of loose skin behind his elbows pinched in the girth. It is therefore not surprising that some horses do not enjoy being tacked-up. It must be done properly if it is to be pleasant; nor must it ever be hurried if proper care is to be taken.

Small children trying to tack-up large ponies should have an upturned feed tin or a small stool to stand on, to enable them to reach properly.

Fitting the bridle

To fit a horse's bridle correctly, the throatlatch and noseband must both be undone first. Holding the bridle in the left hand, and standing at the horse's near-side, first slip the reins gently over his head and rest them half-way down his neck. Then pass your right arm around the back of his head and take the bridle by the cheeks into your right hand and draw it up his face until the bit lies next to his lips (*see* photograph page 54 left). Your right hand should be resting on the bridge of his nose to keep him from tossing his head up. Ask him to open his mouth by slipping your left thumb into his mouth and pressing on the bars, i.e., the area of his gums that has no teeth, in the gap between the incisors and molars. When he opens it, gently lift the bridle and slip the bit past his teeth with the left hand, being careful not to bash them.

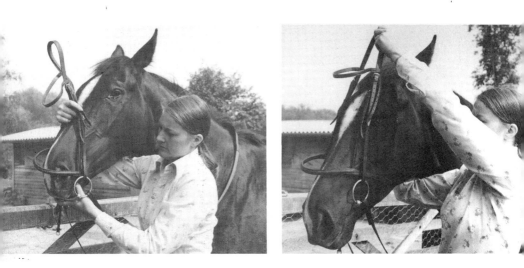

Left With your right hand holding both the cheeks of the bridle and your horse's nose, he will be unable to put his head up and evade having his bit put in.

Right Slip the off-side ear into the bridle first, minding the horse's eyes as you pull the bridle back.

When the bit is in his mouth, transfer the bridle to your left hand, holding it by the headpiece, being careful not to let the bit drop from his mouth. Then with the right hand still under his head, reach up and carefully slip his off-side ear into the bridle and bringing your hand back around to the near-side, carefully put his near-side ear under the headpiece also. (*See* photographs above).

Now that the bridle is in place, see that his forelock is moved from underneath the browband to lie on top of it, and that the mane is parted neatly underneath the headpiece so that it is comfortable. It is a good idea to clip away about 2.5cm (1in) of mane where the headpiece lies to make sure that the hair cannot pull. This should be trimmed up, either with scissors or the clippers, once a month, depending on its growth rate, but be careful not to clip more than 2.5cm (1in) or so, otherwise it will make an unsightly gap in the mane, a drawback when you want to plait.

The throatlatch should now be fastened, tight enough for you to be able to fit your clenched fist under it next to the horse's cheek, when his head is in the normal position for riding; (*see* photograph opposite, right) and then fasten the noseband, which must lie

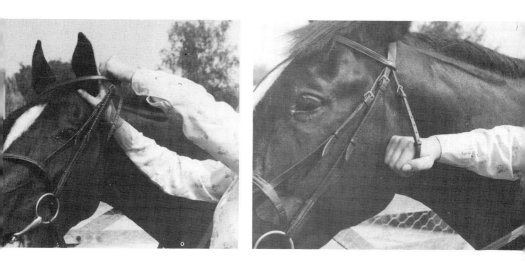

Left This horse has very large ears so I have to be extra careful not to squash them when slipping them under the headpiece.

Right Test the correct fit of the throatlatch. Too loose and it will flap against your horse's face and annoy him. Too tight and it will be very uncomfortable.

underneath the cheekpieces on both sides, leaving enough room to fit two fingers under it on the bridge of the nose (*see* page 56 left). If you are using a curb bit, straighten out the curb chain so that it lies flat against the chin groove before you fasten it, tight enough so that when the pressure of the reins is applied, the chain comes into action when the bit is at an angle of 45° to the vertical (*see* page 56 right).

Now check that the bridle is fitting comfortably. See that it is not lopsided, that the noseband is straight and that the browband is not too tight and neither pinching the horse's ears nor pressing too hard on his forehead. See that the bit is lying at the correct height in the mouth, not down between the teeth nor pinching his lips. If you stand in front of the horse and put your thumbs under the cheekpieces, you can tell if it is too tight (no 'give' at all), or too loose (too much 'give'). The photograph (page 57 left) shows the correct amount of 'give' that you should be able to feel when the bit is at the right level.

Some horses refuse to open their mouths for the bit, especially youngsters, so a little honey or molasses smeared across it will make it more acceptable. It is quite safe to put your thumb right into the horse's mouth in the area of the bars, where there are no teeth, and if

55

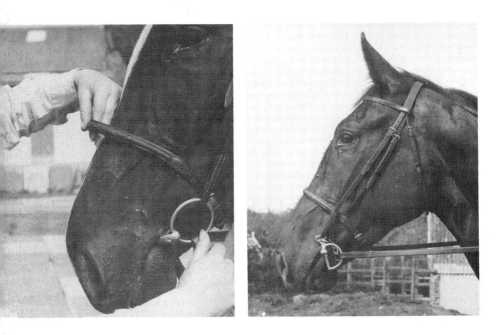

Left A cavesson noseband should allow for two fingers to fit between it and the horse's nose. A drop noseband should allow one finger only, otherwise it will be ineffective.

Right A Kimblewick bit correctly fitted showing the curb chain coming into action as the reins draw the bit back to the angle of 45°.

you press down on his tongue, he should open his mouth for you. At this moment, however, he may try to push his head up as a resistance, but your right hand will be holding the bridle and the bridge of the nose (*see* page 54 left), which will prevent him doing so.

A reward of pony nuts may be given when the bridle is on, but this habit should be faded out once the horse is accepting his bridle properly.

To remove the bridle correctly, undo the throatlatch and the noseband, also the curb chain if there is one. Take the reins gently over the head, then put your right arm under the horse's head and your hand on his nose – the same way as for putting on the bridle. Take hold of the bridle by the head piece with your left hand and gently pull it forward from the horse's face, carefully freeing the ears one at a time (*see* photograph opposite right). At this point, be sure

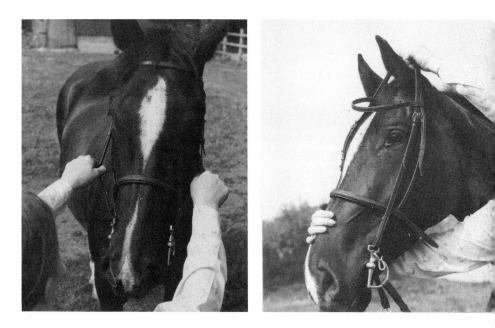

Left Check that the bridle is fitted properly. There must be sufficient 'give' in the cheekpieces, as shown, or the bridle is too tight.

Right Place one hand on the horse's nose when taking the bridle off so that he cannot throw his head up.

to keep a steady hold on the nose, otherwise, if the horse throws up his head, he will catch the bit around his incisor teeth and hurt his mouth. If this happens, he will probably run back and get loose with the bit still in his teeth and the bridle on the ground under his feet. Apart from ruining the bridle, this experience will upset the horse and may hurt his mouth badly.

Fitting the saddle

Next comes the saddle, which is relatively easy to fit, but must still be put on properly. Have the saddle ready to put on the horse, i.e., with the stirrup irons run up under the leathers and the girth lying across the waist of the saddle and attached to the girth straps on the off-side. Stand on the near-side of the horse, and place it gently on his back, just forward of its normal position and slide it back the last

5cm (2in). This little procedure ensures that the hairs of his coat are smoothed in the correct direction, i.e., front to back, with the lie of the coat. Pushing the saddle forward if it is too far back will ruffle the hairs and make the horse uncomfortable.

Walk around to the off-side, having got this far, and pull down the girth. Never push it over the top from the near-side, as it will hit the horse's legs. Check that the girth is not twisted and that the sweat flap (if there is one) is not tucked up under the panel, instead of lying correctly under the girth buckles.

Back again at the near-side, reach underneath for the girth and fasten it, lightly to begin with. Never pull the girth up tight straight away, even if you wish to ride almost immediately. Allow the horse's back to become accustomed to the saddle before tightening it

Put the saddle on gently, just forward of the normal position. Slide it back into place smoothing the lie of the coat.

further, especially if he is clipped and the saddle is cold. Doing the girth up in stages will ensure that your horse will not come to object to it. Having done it up, run your fingers down between the girth and the chest on both sides of the horse, to be sure that no hairs are being pulled, nor the skin pinched. If a nylon string girth is used, this is especially important, to prevent galling on these very sensitive areas of skin – one good reason for horses not liking their saddles put on. Nylon and string girths should be washed regularly, to ensure that they do not become hard and caked with sweat and mud.

The best type of girth is a leather one, and although more expensive, will last for years if carefully looked after, and is far more comfortable for the horse and much safer than a cheap girth. Balding, three-fold and Atherstone are the most common leather girths in use, and they should be wiped over with a damp cloth each time they are used. Regular applications of saddle soap and occasional leather oil will keep girths supple, but remember to check the stitching around the buckles regularly and have them re-stitched by the saddler when they begin to wear.

During the winter, when ponies grow long woolly coats, it is difficult to smooth the hair under the girth just by running the fingers down under it. This can easily be done by lifting up each of the forelegs in turn and pulling them forward (*see* photograph page 60).

Do not forget to check that the girth is tight enough before you mount; some horses blow themselves out when being tacked-up. Remember to tighten it again if necessary when you have been mounted for a few minutes and the horse has relaxed.

Some horses have 'cold backs'. A horse who suffers with this when first mounted will appear to collapse in the middle and may stagger forward with his hindquarters trembling. This condition can be caused by getting straight on to a clipped horse that has only just had the saddle put on, and naturally enough shrinks away from it as it is so cold pressing down on his warm back. It can, however, occur at any time once the horse has acquired the habit. When you first mount such a horse, do not sit down in the saddle, but stay up on your knees with your weight in the stirrups and walk him around for a minute or so until he settles. If you want to clip a horse that is 'cold-backed', either leave a patch of hair unclipped under the saddle, or use a numnah. Anyhow, avoid putting the saddle on when it is cold, by keeping it in the house if possible. If you must put it on cold, then tack-up at least ten minutes before you ride and put the

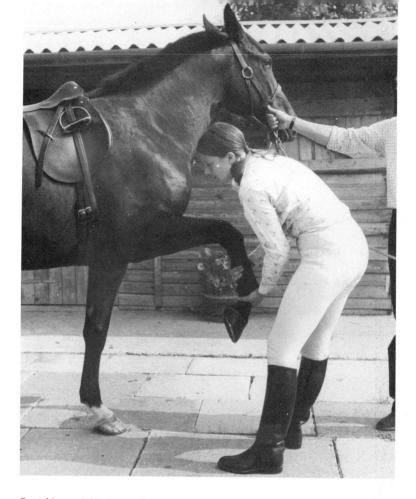

Stretching each foreleg out thus, when the girth is fastened, will ensure that the skin is not being pinched behind the elbows. It will also smooth the lie of the hair.

rugs back on top of it so that the horse has a chance to warm it up.

If a horse should kick out or try to bite when being saddled the only reason is that he has suffered in the past from some of the painful experiences above – girth galls being the most common. If he tries to bite, he should be tied up to have his tack put on and not be unduly reprimanded for trying to bite the manger, walls, etc.; but he should be soothed and quietly handled, and have his saddle put on carefully as described. Do the girth up very carefully and in slow stages so that he is not annoyed by it. Be careful not to get kicked by standing too close to the quarters. In time, with gentle handling and the occasional reward when the saddle is on, the horse will come to realize that he is not going to be hurt and should calm down. Never strike him or lose your temper if he tries to bite or kick, just use a sharp word and then talk quietly again to him to reassure him.

Girth galls
It is easy to prevent girth galls forming, but difficult to get rid of them once they have formed. They are most likely to occur if a dirty girth is used, or when the horse is unfit and his skin soft, as in the case of hunters just up from their summer holiday at grass. The application of surgical spirit to the girth area twice daily will help to harden off the skin quickly and help prevent their occurrence. Regular attention to this area at grooming time is essential and particularly before rugging-up after riding, to see that mud and sweat are removed before the roller is put on.

If your horse has girth galls, he must not be ridden until they are completely healed, as the girth will only rub and make them worse. They should be bathed with saline solution (warm water with salt added) then dried, and wound powder (sulphanilomide) or an ointment such as Savlon should be applied. Do not use Vaseline as it prevents air getting to the girth galls and thereby slows down healing. Strong disinfectants such as Dettol are not to be recommended either, as they also damage the rate of new tissue growth. When the girth galls have healed, a tubular length of sheepskin may be passed over the girth to help keep the skin trouble free until it has had the chance to harden off, but this must be kept scrupulously clean and soft if it is to be useful and not harmful. Prevention is the best cure as always.

Mounting
There is no excuse for a horse not standing still to be mounted, although his handling is usually to blame. This fault generally takes the form of the horse walking off before the rider is properly aboard, or running back or circling round the rider when he is trying to get on.

Walking off
The first problem, that of moving off before the rider is settled in the saddle, usually results from the horse having been allowed to walk on before being asked to do so, instead of always being made to stand

still until the rider has adjusted his girth and stirrups. Such bad manners develop because of lack of thought on the rider's part; and will worsen if not corrected, until the horse is beginning to move off as soon as the rider puts his left foot in the iron. By this stage, he will have become difficult to mount and the rider, if he loses his temper, may jab the horse with the reins or hit him for not keeping still. This will, of course, come as a shock to the horse, who has previously been allowed to walk on virtually when he wanted to. Such treatment at this stage could lead on to the second problem mentioned above, running back when the rider tries to mount, only this time the cause will probably be fear of being hit or jabbed in the mouth when the rider gets on. The horse who is dead keen to move off may start the habit of circling around the rider as he tries to put a foot in the stirrup, especially if he is prevented from going forward by the rider holding the reins tightly.

Obviously, all these problems could be avoided with a little forethought. Whenever a horse is mounted, he should be made to stand still for a few seconds, as a matter of course, in the name of good manners, until asked to move off; this will prevent bad habits developing.

It is not enough to have an assistant hold the horse still for you when you mount in the yard; this will not teach him to stand still when there is no assistant. In any case, you may have to dismount and mount again whilst out riding alone; and the bigger the horse, the more difficult it will be to get on him again.

To re-school the horse that moves off too quickly, find a suitable place to mount, where he cannot step forward. A corner of the schooling area, if you have one at your disposal, is an ideal place (providing that it is a fenced-in area). Begin by lungeing the horse (with saddle and bridle on) to be sure he understands the voice commands you will use, i.e., 'stand' and 'walk-on'. Once these are established clearly, take off the cavesson and lead your horse to the chosen corner of the school and make him stand quietly while you run down the irons and check your girth. If he attempts to move or sidle around, then quietly push him back into place and say firmly 'stand'. When you are ready to mount, gather up the reins firmly, so that you have sufficient control of his head to stop him turning, and place your left foot in the stirrup. At this point he will probably try to move, if he has not already done so. Repeat the command 'stand' and take your foot out of the stirrup. When he is settled, take the stirrup again, talking to him all the while, but if he moves, take your foot down, say 'stand', and push him back into place. Repeat this procedure until he understands that your are not going to get on him until he does stand still. Do not lose your temper, however, as he certainly will not understand that. Be patient and give clear instructions so he does not become muddled. When he has at last stood still and you have mounted, make him stand still for a few seconds before you say 'walk-on', and apply the leg. You must use this voice aid to begin with, so that he will learn that 'stand' applies until you say 'walk-on', the same as when he is being lunged.

Now ride him around the school for a few minutes, then bring him to halt by the corner used to mount him, and say 'stand'. Dismount and give him a pat. Prepare to mount again and repeat the procedure as before.

When you have completed this exercise several times, take your horse out for his hack or work. Do not make the mistake of repeating the exercise too often the first time you do it, as the horse may begin to fidget simply from boredom. Repeat the whole procedure for several days and make a transition from using the corner of the school to mounting and dismounting anywhere around the perimeter.

If you do not have a schooling area to use, a gate, or a wall of the stable will serve to stop the horse from stepping forward; however, if you use a gate, make sure it is not at the opposite end of the yard from your normal exit, or the horse will merely whip round as you try to mount, in order to be away down the yard and off on his ride! Make certain that whichever place you choose to teach your horse to stand still, you will have the horse at your best advantage, and not vice versa.

Running back

If your horse runs back when you try to get on, you will need to reverse the method of re-schooling described, and stand the horse with his bottom in a corner or against a hedge or wall so he cannot step back. If his running back is caused by a fear of being hit, you must be careful that when you have him cornered like this he does not rear as you step forward to get on. Speak to him in soothing tones and stroke his neck and shoulder. If necessary, to begin with, have someone to help you hold him and give him a handful of nuts while you mount, as quietly as possible. If the horse does attempt to rear and your helper tries to hold him down, he may panic and either leap forward, or go higher and go over backwards. If he tries to go up, the reins should be released at once and he should be calmed and reassured. Only patience and reward will solve this problem, but it should not take very long, once you have gained the horse's confidence.

Circling round

The horse who runs round you in circles because he is keen to be off may also be held by an assistant to begin with, as he will need to be kept straight. He must also be taught the commands 'stand' and 'walk-on' and must be made to stand still once you are mounted for at least half a minute to teach him some patience. To foil him, practise mounting and dismounting for a couple of days, but not taking him out for exercise or working him at all. His keenness will therefore diminish slightly and when he has begun to improve his manners and least expects it, take him out for a ride.

It is very easy to let your horse fall into bad habits like these, especially when you are in a hurry, but it is always worth taking time to teach good manners. If you intend to show your horse in a class where he will be ridden by a judge, he will lose valuable points for manners if he will not stand still, and if the judge cannot get on without an awful fuss, he may well refuse to ride your horse at all. If he is a local judge, he will remember you both at the next show, and your horse will automatically be marked down unless his manners have improved radically.

6 Bad habits when leading and riding out

Leading

It may not seem at first that leading badly is a serious fault; but there will probably come a time when you will have trouble if your horse does not lead properly. If he does not walk beside you, but trails along behind when you are on foot, you might be stepped on if something frightens him and he jumps forward; or he may even knock you down – either way, you may be hurt. When being led, he should walk slightly in front of you, so that you are at a level with his shoulder. Also he should lead properly from both the near-side and the off-side, otherwise you will have a problem if you are going to lead two horses at once, and neither is used to being led from the off-side. If they are both allowed to walk along behind you and one threatens or bites the other, you could easily lose hold of both of them in the ensuing fracas.

In winter, or indeed at any time of year, exercising two horses by riding one and leading the other may be necessary, and the horse being led must be wise to this or it will be almost an impossible task. If he hangs back, he may be kicked; or he may try to bite the horse you are riding; in either event you may lose hold of him. Again, if he is startled by something, you will not have sufficient control unless you can keep him up alongside you.

When riding on the road, you should ride with the traffc, and keep the horse's head bent slightly towards the road. Never turn your horse's head towards the hedge; he may swing his quarters out into the road if he cannot see what is coming up behind him. When riding one horse and leading another, the led horse must always be on the kerb side so that he is sheltered from the traffic. If he is led on the traffic side, he could easily get hit by simply swinging out his hindquarters, over which you will have no control.

When leading a horse on the road on foot, you should walk into the oncoming traffic in the opposite direction to the traffic flow. Again, the horse should be on the kerb side, so that he is shielded from the traffic by you, and unable to swing out into the road. Horses should never be ridden or led on the pavement. Apart from the risk of them fouling the footpath, which is irresponsible, and the possibility of inconvenience and danger to pedestrians, a horse is quite likely to actually jump out into the road if he is startled by something in a garden, or a car suddenly coming out of a gateway in front of him, which could be disastrous.

Teaching a foal to lead
To start right at the beginning, foals should be taught to lead properly from the age of only a few days. It can be dangerous for the foal, and it is also lazy, to lead only the mare and allow the foal to follow. He will happily do it, but it is at this stage that he should be learning to be led. It is the time when he will be most likely to co-operate, as you will be leading his mother, and he will want to come too. Ideally mares and foals should live in during the day and out at night during the summer months, so that they can rest in the heat of the day away from the flies, and graze in peace at night. This being the case, it is a good idea to lead the mare and foal on alternate sides morning and evening, so that the foal does not become one-sided, but learns to lead from either side as a matter of course. To begin with, when teaching the foal to lead, you will need an assistant to lead the mare so that you can concentrate entirely on the foal.

If you start with him young enough, you should be able to control him easily. Once he starts to get big and strong, he may put up more of a fight. To begin with, lead him beside his mother, slightly towards her hindquarters, which is the natural place for him to be, as you will notice when they are out together and the foal is following his mother. As well as having a rope attached to the foal slip, it is a good idea to place a second rope around his quarters, then pass the end of it through the rope clip. You will then only have to hold one end of it, and if the foal will not step forward, pull gently on it so it tightens a little and puts pressure on his bottom, which will make him step forward. Never try to drag a foal by the foal slip. He may stand right up and fall over, or suddenly leap forward on top of you. The use of the second rope means that he will learn to lead gently from the hand as he will be 'pushed' (by the second rope behind his quarters),

66

rather than 'pulled' along (by the rope on the foal slip). Foals learn to lead very quickly by this method, and within a few days, it will be possible for you to lead both the mare and her foal without the help of an assistant. (*See* photographs pages 42 and 43).

Re-training a horse to lead

If you have a horse that will not lead properly beside you, either from another or when you are on foot, you can quite easily re-train him.

To begin with, your horse should understand the basic voice commands 'walk-on', and either 'halt' or 'whoa', whichever you use when lungeing or riding him. You will need to carry a stick to begin with – a dressage whip being the ideal length – and start by standing at the horse's shoulder on the nearside. Hold the headcollar rope in your right hand, approximately 15cm (6in) from the clip and hold the other end of the rope and the dressage whip in your left hand. Incidentally, never coil a headcollar rope around your hand. In an emergency, if the horse pulled it tight, your fingers could be broken. When you are ready to move off, say 'walk-on' firmly and clearly, and at the same time, tap the horse with the whip, using it as you would if you were mounted, i.e., behind your left side. If necessary, repeat the command and touch him with the whip again until he steps forward. He must learn to lead on ahead of you, so you must not step forward first. You will need to keep repeating the command and touching him with the whip to keep him ahead until he gets used to the idea, and if all goes well, leading him from the near-side; then you can swop over the off-side and try again. Be careful not to confuse the horse to begin with, and if he is not going very well for you, stay on the near-side until he has mastered it properly before changing over. (*See* photograph page 41).

To teach the horse to stay alongside while led from another horse is a little more complicated; you will need a mounted assistant as well as another horse to ride yourself. The assistant should ride beside but slightly behind the led horse, on his near-side, and keep him going forward by touching him with a whip while you give the voice commands, 'walk-on' and 'trot-on' (which should sound 'ter-rot'). Do not try to carry the whip yourself as this will only make him shy away from you, which is the opposite of what you want. You would probably run out of hands trying to do three things at once in any case. As you proceed, change pace up and down from trot to walk and so on; and as soon as the horse improves and begins to keep up steadily, the assistant can stop using the whip. He should stay in place nonetheless to give an occasional reminder if necessary.

For the subsequent few outings, it will still be necessary to have a rider behind the 'ride and lead' pair just as an insurance policy until the horse's obedience is firmly established. In addition to this procedure, the horse should also be lunged for a few minutes each day to firmly instil the voice commands into his mind, but the commands used must be identical for both lungeing and leading; and the same person should teach the horse for both, so there is no risk of confusing him.

Shying

Shying is probably one of the most dangerous vices, as most horses who shy do it when out on the roads; and as even country roads carry quite heavy traffic these days, the dangers are obvious. True shying is caused by fear and is not to be confused with napping, which is basically plain disobedience. However, a horse can shy anywhere and at any time, so you should always keep one eye ahead for approaching trouble.

Some horses have bad eyesight, unbeknown to their owners, and they will shy at the same things every day, even though it becomes apparent that they are not in the least frightened. If a horse cannot see properly, the distorted images he does see will confuse him until, on approaching, they become clearer. In these cases it is worth having his eyes checked by a veterinary surgeon to make sure his sight is not defective.

Most instances of shying take place out on the roads because there are more unnatural things around for the horse to shy at. Young horses are prone to this habit through lack of experience of life. Obviously, when youngsters are first ridden out in traffic, it will be an advantage to have them follow an older horse who behaves well and will set a good example, until they learn that there is really nothing to fear.

The golden rule when a horse is trying to shy at something is to turn his head away from it and not look at it yourself. Close your legs on him and drive him forward, talking quietly to him. Never try to make him approach the object so that 'he can have a good look at it'. He obviously does not want a good look, or he would not be trying to shy. The more fuss you make, the more you will convince the horse that there really is something to be terrified about. The more relaxed you are and the more quietly you sit in the saddle the better. If you tense up and get flustered you will directly communicate your feelings to the horse, who will probably panic. Remember that the horse's natural instinctive reaction to anything he fears is to run away from it as fast as he can, but you must teach him to be bold and to trust your judgment.

If you see or hear something up ahead that he might shy at – like plastic sheeting in the hedge, or something noisy like a tractor coming around the corner, do not collect the horse up at once, or he will immediately become aware that something is about to happen. You will have put him on his guard – ready to panic at any moment. You should always ride out with a good contact on your horse's mouth and your legs in contact with his sides and it should therefore not be necessary to gather him up.

Do not look at the plastic sheeting or frightening object yourself, just reassure your horse with your voice and gently turn his head away. Send him forward quietly and pretend to him that there is nothing to worry about.

Talk to him all the while, telling him not to be a silly boy, but be fairly firm with your aids, because, if he is an obedient horse, his desire to please you may help to overcome his desire to turn tail and run for cover.

If your horse is bad with lorries or heavy traffic, put your hand up to warn the driver. Most lorry drivers are very considerate and if you remember to smile and thank them for their trouble as you pass, they will continue to be so. If you are really having trouble getting your horse to pass a lorry, the driver may even switch the engine off for you, but watch out when you have passed, as he may release his air brakes with a resounding 'p-tssss'.

It is possible to buy tunic-type over-jackets for you to wear, some with slogans such as 'CAUTION – NERVOUS HORSE' and 'CAUTION – YOUNG HORSE' printed in large black letters on an orange fluorescent background. These are available through most good saddlers or by mail order through magazines such as *Horse & Hound*. They are a very good idea, as they warn motorists to be careful when passing you; however, it is still up to you to ride sensibly and not attempt to ride through busy high streets for example, expecting everyone to keep out of your way. (*See* photograph page 44).

Napping

Napping is a little different and stems more often from disobedience or too much food and too little exercise, the quickest way to make a horse play up. Horses also tend to nap when they have you at your worst disadvantage and may use napping as a trick to play on you if they are allowed to get away with it. You will need to drive the horse forward smartly with your legs and voice and you should always carry a whip, as legs and voice alone may not be sufficient. Spurs may also be worn, to begin with, to teach the horse to go forward when he is told; firm riding is the only way to cure a horse from napping. If you ride your horse actively and keep his mind occupied by varying not only the pace and content of his work, but also the places where you take him, he is far less likely to pick up napping as a habit.

Napping may develop into rearing, which can be dangerous (*see* page 76), so it is important not to let it continue and get worse.

Jogging

Jogging is a most annoying habit. While it is a little difficult to cure, this can be achieved in the end by re-schooling. It is not really a true disobedience, as it occurs most often in horses who are very keen rides; but it can be an evasion in a short-strided horse who is too lazy to walk out, and the problem will be increased by a rider who is too lazy to make him. Horses most often start jogging when ridden in company, especially if they are behind other horses who walk out well, with whom they are unable to keep up easily; so it is no good expecting to start re-schooling under such circumstances.

Jogging is also very wearing for the horse and may cause him to lose condition. Even if he is comfortable when jogging along, he is doing damage to himself, not to mention the extra wear to his shoes, and he should therefore be taught to walk properly.

In the re-schooling of a horse who jogs incessantly, the voice plays a major role. To begin with, lungeing him and making sure he understands the voice commands clearly is of paramount importance. When you lunge him, do not use side-reins as they will discourage him from lengthening his stride, which is just what you will want him to do. When you ask him to trot on, make sure that he performs a good active trot, never a jog-trot. See that he is using his back and hocks properly and that he is tracking-up. This means that his hind feet should fall into the tracks made by the front feet, and whether they do or not will show you whether your horse is working correctly. When you bring him back to walk, have him walk out in a well-established swinging stride with a good even rhythm.

When you have established good control over him on the lunge, you can begin to ride out, but to begin with, you must ride on your own so that your horse will not have another horse to compete with. Allow him sufficient freedom of his head and neck so that he can stretch out. Relax in the saddle and ask him to step out a little more with each stride. Keep a sufficient contact on his mouth so that he does not break stride, but remember that too firm a contact may cause him to overbend, a common fault in keen horses who are often kept on a tight rein; it is very difficult to make a horse 'take rein' once this situation develops.

Your legs should stay in contact with his sides at all times so that when you apply them, they do not come as a shock and send him forward into a jog. When he does start to jog, which he will soon enough, close your fingers on the reins, resist gently, squeeze gently with your legs and at the same time say 'walk' firmly. Say it with a downward inflection of the voice and draw the word out as you would when lungeing so that it sounds – 'wa-a-alk'. Then send him forward with the leg and ask him to step out again. Repeat this procedure every time he breaks stride, but, above all, be patient. It may take a long while before you can teach him to walk out, especially if his conformation makes it difficult to extend his stride; but very soon you should be able to anticipate him breaking stride and be able to stop him by closing your fingers and squeezing before he actually jogs on. When you want to trot, make sure that you ask him to trot on. Never let him trot on if he breaks into a jog of his own accord, or you will be condoning his changing pace without your permission.

As previously mentioned, jogging is most often found in horses who are very keen rides; however, it is a fallacy to assume that giving them a good gallop will settle them down. It will have exactly the opposite effect and they will jog more than ever from the excitement. If your horse is a keen ride, he may be over-active in all his paces, and the trot is a very important pace to control, from both a physical and mental point of view. To allow a horse to trot fast and hurry along is a mistake; firstly because he may overreach himself; secondly, it will make him sweat but will not make him use his back or hocks as he would in a controlled pace; thirdly and possibly most important, is that he will be rushing, hurrying and very unsettled and will be in the wrong frame of mind to calm down and walk properly again when asked. If you are to teach him to walk quietly you will need to tone down his whole approach to being ridden, so that he becomes altogether calmer and a more pleasing ride.

As mentioned above, begin his re-training by riding out alone, as it will be much easier for you. When you do ride out in company again, go with someone who is happy to let you take the lead, so that your horse will not be looking to get in front all the time. If your companion has a horse or pony smaller than yours, so much the better, as they will not have to hold back in order to let you stay in walk. Do not go riding with someone with a huge Thoroughbred, as they will undoubtedly get fed up with having to mince along behind you.

If you have to ride out in a group, and your horse jogs on, ask him to trot properly for a few strides, not jog, until he catches up sufficiently and then ask him to walk again. Never just let him jog on complacently. Once you have taught him to walk out on his own, you must progress to making him walk out in company; but all this will take perseverance and pure determination on your part.

Attempting to roll when being ridden
Occasionally a horse may attempt to roll while he is being ridden.

The first possible reason that springs to mind is the horse's desire to rid himself of his rider or saddle, and to have a good roll because he is uncomfortable in his back. This may be on account of ill-fitting tack or because of being overheated, such as during a long summer's afternoon when he is working fairly hard and has become sticky through sweating. This may be compounded if he is wearing a sheepskin numnah, when his saddle may feel to him like a great, hot poultice which he will want to dislodge. As discomfort is probably the most common cause of him trying to roll, be careful to see that the saddle and the numnah, if you use one, are both correctly fitted every time you put them on, and that the horse's back has not been rubbed. Check also for insect bites, which will usually leave tell-tale raised areas on the skin, causing irritation if they come into contact with the saddle.

The desire to roll often occurs when the horse finds himself in water, i.e., when crossing a ford or river, but it may happen if he is merely asked to paddle through a large puddle. Usually the horse will lower his head and begin to paw the ground, splashing the water and you will feel him begin to tremble at the knees. He may however go down without any warning. If you feel that he is about to get down and roll, then quickly raise his head to prevent him from collapsing his forehand. Loud use of the voice combined with strong use of the legs and stick may stop him; if it does, then get him out of the water quickly as he may try to do it again. (*See* photograph page 77.)

If he does go down in spite of your efforts, try and throw yourself clear so that you do not end up underneath him; and if your presence of mind is such, try and dismount on the side opposite from where his legs will be, to avoid being kicked. Obviously if your horse rolls over, he may easily break your saddle; and any rolling whilst wearing it may damage it. Try and get him up as quickly as possible by using your voice, and your stick if you have not dropped it. If you still have hold of the reins, use them to stop him putting his head to the ground as he needs to do this, and also to use his neck, in order to roll on to his back.

This problem of trying to roll may only happen on an isolated occasion; but if it is not properly dealt with, it may develop into a habit which will be quite dangerous to the rider and expensive in repairing and replacing damaged tack. Remember that the horse can only get down when he is stationary and will usually do it carefully and quite slowly to avoid bumping himself heavily, so you should find that you have time to drive him forward. If he repeatedly tries to go down, be sure to keep his head up and strongly voice your objection to his behaviour until he gives up the idea.

Pulling

A horse who pulls continuously when being ridden is not a pleasure to ride. If the habit of pulling is not checked and dealt with correctly it can develop into the most serious of vices under saddle, bolting.

A horse learns to pull for several reasons, most of which stem from his being unhappy with his bit for some reason. A novice rider who leans on the reins for his balance will undoubtedly upset a horse with a soft mouth, as will a careless rider using his hands roughly. The horse's mouth is very sensitive and he can quickly become frightened of his bridle. Unfortunately for him, his natural reaction to anything he fears is to run away from it and this is usually what he does – he pulls at the bit to get away from it. The more a horse pulls, the more likely he is to find himself fitted with a more severe bit. He reacts by pulling harder and as the habit gets worse, his mouth will become harder and his neck stronger, until he is impossible to stop.

Unfortunately, many riders are virtually taught to kick for 'go' and pull for 'stop'. This may be ideal for the riding school horse who is likely to be quiet and a bit slow and probably only too pleased to stop. However, any spirited horse who is fit and keen will need to be ridden with tact and a light touch if the rider is not to find himself locked in battle with the horse galloping flat out. The horse's mouth is very delicate and must be handled with care; riders should be taught from the start to use the leg more and the hands less. If you do not pull against a horse, he cannot pull at you.

Some riders gather up the reins too short and take a firm hold, before, for example, they strike off for canter, and this is where the battle begins. If the rider takes a hold of the bit, so can the horse, and a physical battle of strength with any horse will see the rider coming off second-best. You should have sufficient contact on the reins when trotting for you to shorten the reins only a little when you wish to canter; but it should not be necessary to increase the amount of contact, which should remain light. If the horse begins to hurry along, the contact of both leg and hand should be increased, with the rider sitting quietly in the saddle. If the horse starts to pull at the bit, the rider should resist by pulling one rein and then the other in a give-and-take action. Never take a dead pull with both reins at once. The horse is much stronger and can easily pull you out of the saddle, making you lose your balance. At this point, he will have the advantage of being able to increase his speed before you have recovered your position.

If he is really set alight and will not listen to you, shorten your reins, get your knees into the saddle and pull the right rein down over the near-side of the horse's neck. At the same time, bring your left hand right up as high as you can (*see* photograph page 78 above). You should be able to stop the worst puller in this way, even if he is only wearing a snaffle.

There are, of course, other reasons for a horse becoming a puller. Too much food and not enough exercise will make him a very keen ride. If he is ridden by an inexperienced or nervous rider, he may find it very easy to take off whenever he wants to without being checked effectively.

Correct tack
An ill-fitting bridle which is too tight, or too small a bit which may pinch the mouth are two other common causes, so it is important to

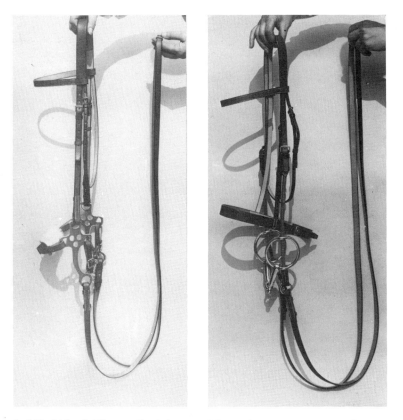

Left The bitless bridle, as well as being a possible solution for a puller, can also be used if a horse has a mouth injury but must be ridden out anyway. Have some instruction in the correct way to use it, as it is different from riding in an ordinary bridle.

Right The gag snaffle is designed to raise the horse's head when the reins are pulled, and may cure the puller who goes off with his head down. This is a Salisbury gag.

see that tack fits properly, and is suitable for the horse.

The different types of bit that can be tried are too numerous to list, but if you can borrow different ones to try out, you may be lucky enough to find one your horse is happy wearing, if a plain snaffle is clearly no longer strong enough for him. If he puts his head down to pull, you may find that a gag snaffle will help (*see* photograph above). This will have a lifting effect on the head, as the bit slides up the cheekpieces when the reins are pulled. On the other hand, if the horse puts his head right up and gets above the point of control, try him in a standing or running martingale which, fitted correctly, will keep his head from being raised so high.

If the horse's mouth has really been spoiled and you cannot bit him successfully a bitless bridle may be your answer. There are several types, all designed to put pressure on the nose, the chin and the poll. It is just as important to fit a bitless bridle correctly as it is to fit one with a bit; if it is fitted too high, it will be ineffective; and if too low, i.e., on the soft cartilage at the base of the nose, it may obstruct the horse's breathing. Learn to use it correctly.

Many horses who are impossible to bit successfully due to their mouths having been spoiled will go happily in a bitless bridle, so it is well worth trying one. They are quite expensive, so if you can borrow one to begin with, so much the better.

Bolting

Unfortunately, however, there are horses who develop the habit of pulling to such an extent that they find out that their strength is far superior than that of the rider and this can lead to them bolting. When a horse bolts, he gallops blindly at top speed without fear or care for his own safety and this vice can have disastrous and sometimes even fatal results for both horse and rider. The horse who learns to do this is best destroyed as there is no cure for it. However, if the horse is a mare or an entire male horse, she or he may be used for breeding purposes if their general temperament is good and they are of outstanding conformation.

Rearing

Rearing is one of the most feared of vices, but it is not as dangerous as it is reputed. It is perfectly natural for a horse to stand up on his hind legs and it is surprising how well he can balance in this posture. The only thing which will unbalance him sufficiently for him to go over backwards is the rider pulling him over; and it is the fear of this happening that makes most riders' blood run cold. Because we rarely come across horses who rear, we do not get the chance to learn how to ride them, or indeed how to cope when a horse does go up.

Rearing is usually practised as an evasion from the rider's leg and is a deliberate resistance on the part of the horse, the trouble can start by a horse not being made to go forward obediently from the leg and can begin with the horse napping.

This mare is just about to go down and roll in the ford. Her rider must quickly get her head up and drive her forward out of the water.

The 'One hand up and the other over and down' method is worth trying if you are really getting 'carted'. Ideally, shorten your reins first, if you have time.

If your horse kicks, keep clear of other horses and put a red ribbon on his tail as a warning. Fasten it securely and comfortably.

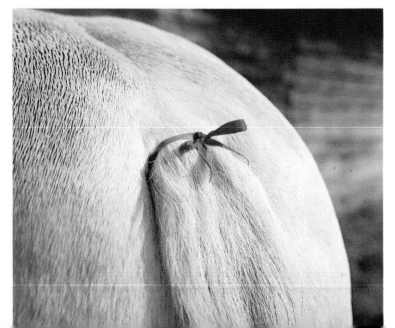

Loading: one assistant will be leading the horse and the other two should hold one line each, straight outwards from the back of the trailer. Make the trailer appear more inviting by swinging the back of the partition away to one side, which will also give you more room to manoeuvre.

The two assistants change sides behind the horse, criss-crossing the lines at the level of the horse's second thighs. Encourage your horse to keep his head down by offering nuts in a bowl held down and forward of his nose. Only let him take some as he progresses up the ramp.

Cementing trust and friendship with your horse is the first step towards a happy and successful partnership.

Once the horse learns that he is not going to be made to do as he is told, he may try out a few 'tricks', and rearing is one of them. It usually starts with a small half-rear which is not at all unseating, but the rider must immediately send the horse forward with vigorous use of the leg and voice, and the whip if necessary. This first instance may happen when you are approaching something like a small ditch that you would like to jump, and the horse, knowing that it is there, may try to turn away, even though it may only be tiny and well within his scope. So far it is no more than a refusal to co-operate; but if the rider is frightened and gives in to the horse, turning back without another word, the next time will be worse; and there will undoubtedly be a next time. The problem will quickly develop into a vice and the rears will get bigger and bolder.

Very few horses will rear right up on their hind legs, like stallions fighting; but when they do go up the most important thing is to give with the reins immediately. If the reins are used by the rider to hang on with, the horse will go higher and may then be pulled off balance and over backwards. The moment the horse rears, the rider should grip with his knees and bend forward at the waist. (Only if the horse starts to stagger backwards, as though he is losing his balance, need the rider kick his feet clear of the stirrups and slide to the ground). As soon as the horse comes down, he should be calmed and settled, but never driven forward straight away. This would probably result in another rear. The horse should, however, be kept facing the original direction in which he was being ridden; if he has turned around, the hand should be applied gently – again to prevent another resistance. The leg should be applied gently but firmly and an open rein used to lead the horse around to face the right way.

Again, with this habit, prevention is infinitely better than cure, which may obviously prove hazardous to a rider inexperienced with this type of horse. As with other forms of disobedience, in the end it boils down to the horse learning respect for his rider as well as having confidence in him. To cure rearing you must be both tough and tender, and have endless patience and determination.

It is however, foolhardy to ride out alone on a horse who is known to rear, and especially if you do not tell someone exactly where you are going and what time to expect you back. If you can ride out with a friend, even if you wish to ride in front and have your horse going forward obediently on his own, it can be a great help to have a lead from another horse when you do have trouble. When your horse is following obediently behind the other one, you can always go back and repeat the exercise with your horse in front. If you were to tackle him over such a serious problem as rearing whilst out alone, the consequences could be dangerous for you if everything did not go according to plan. Until you are half-way to curing him it is in both your horse's and our own interest to play safe.

Bucking

There is nothing more unseating than a good hard buck, and nothing more likely to unseat you than a series of them. While bucking is a very bad habit, its cause may be the age-old problem of too much food and not enough work, in which case the remedy is simple. Horses love to buck, unfortunately for us, and you have only to turn them loose in the field on a cold winter's morning and watch them let rip to see how much they enjoy it. However, they must learn not to do it when being ridden.

A horse who bucks has one saving grace as far as the rider is concerned, and that is that he will warn you of what he is about to do. You will fell his back come up and see his head go down between his knees just before the explosion and that is the time to get weight into your stirrups and your seat off the saddle before you can be catapulted out of it.

Most horses who buck will do it habitually in the same places every time they are out, or during the first canter or whenever. You will soon know when they are most likely to do it and you can try to prevent it happening. First of all, if the horse cannot get his head down, he cannot buck, or at least, not very hard and so you should keep him on a good contact so as to be ready for him. As soon as he shows any sign of attempting to get his head down, send him forward into a brisk trot and keep his head up. If you are cantering, keep your seat out of the saddle and be ready to lift one hand if his head goes down. It is pointless to pull with both hands as he is so much stronger and you will merely be pulled off balance yourself, but to pull one rein only will send him off balance and spoil his buck.

Some horses may benefit from being lunged for ten minutes before being ridden, especially if they are fit and full of beans, having been standing since the previous day. During this time, they should be allowed to buck freely and loosen up, so side-reins will not be needed.

Some horses buck as a resistance to the whip, and they must be taught to go forward from it. Misuse of the whip, however, is the most common cause of this, in which case the horse is justified in bucking. The whip should be used only as a reinforcement of the leg aid and must be applied in conjunction with your leg and just behind it. Never strike a horse on the stifle or around the quarters as this will more than likely cause him to buck. If your horse will not go forward from the whip, it may be an advantage to wear spurs on him for a while as an extra reinforcement to the leg, when you begin to re-school him, but they must be used with care, and never worn

'Prepare to buck', and, to help you stay aboard, use a short pair of reins and knot the hand part. Then you can balance on the neck with your reins and not get thrown right forward.

upside-down pointing upwards towards the horse's flanks. Only use spurs if you are sufficiently competent.

It is helpful, when you are riding a horse likely to buck, to tie a knot in the end of your reins so that you only leave yourself with about 25cm (10in) of spare leather between your hands. Then when your horse bucks, by keeping one hand either side of his neck, you will be able to support yourself to some extent by the reins held on his withers, and not be flung up and around his neck, as you would if your reins were very long. It will also prevent the horse from getting complete control of his head if the reins are shortened like this, and the more control you can keep over his head, the less he will be able to buck hard. Keep up on your knees and send him forward with your heels and voice. Use your whip as well if you have the confidence to take your reins in one hand and your courage in the other. (*See* photograph page 83.)

7 Kicking and biting

Kicking

This is a nasty vice, whether it is kicking other horses or people, and some horses unfortunately indulge in both. There is little you can do to teach a horse not to kick other horses, but plenty you can do to prevent him from getting the chance.

Mares are often more susceptible to kicking other horses; to a certain extent it is their natural instinct. When you consider horses in their natural environment, the herd consists of one stallion, a number of mares and the youngstock. When the mares come into season, the stallion will mate with them, but should he attempt to come up behind a mare who is not ready to be covered, she will squeal and lash out to show the stallion she does not want his attentions. Stallions in the surroundings of herd life instinctively know the right time and do not get kicked very often. Also the mares will be unshod, and the damage done by a kick from an unshod hoof is minimal compared with that from one which is shod.

So you can see that a mare who is not in season has a natural tendency to lash out when approached from behind; this tendency will vary in degree from a mare who ignores it completely, to one who lays back her ears and lets fly.

If your mare kicks other horses when turned out in the field, it may be necessary to put her out on her own, as you will not be able to stop her from doing it. One solution, if it is practicable, is to have the mares and geldings turned out in separate fields. This is the rule in many yards, because it cuts down the number of injuries that take place during scraps and reduces the chances of horses laming each other.

This habit is not confined to mares, but the majority of kickers are mares, not geldings. The earlier a colt is gelded, the less natural instinct he will develop for being a 'boss horse'. Those who are left until late are often the worst offenders. It is, however, necessary to geld them at the right time – too early, and they may not develop a good neck or indeed much personality – too late and they may be difficult to manage if many stallion instincts have developed. As a rule, geldings are more placid and constant than mares and so are often favoured when buying a horse.

If your horse kicks others when you are riding him, he should be corrected immediately with a sharp stroke of the whip. His instincts may prevent you from teaching him not to kick, so you will need to put a red ribbon in the top of his tail to warn other riders that he is a kicker. It will not be sufficient just to ride him out hunting with a red ribbon in his tail and expect everyone to keep out of his way. It will be your responsibility to make sure that he does not get close enough to kick anyone else's horse, so you should not ride in the middle of the field, but keep to the edge or even to the back. If other horses come up to pass you, turn your horse's head towards them so that his quarters will be moved away. Be very careful not to let him kick a hound – you may well be sent home permanently for such a misdemeanour or at least until you have taught your horse some 'manners'.

When riding in the show ring the same will apply, but as you will obviously not be able to put a red ribbon in your horse's tail, be careful to warn anyone riding behind you not to get too close.

A horse who kicks out at his handler is not a pleasant horse to look after, nor, probably, a very happy horse himself. Thoroughbreds and highly-strung stock often kick out when being groomed or rugged up, but if they do not aim the kicks at you, you may rightly suppose that their high breeding is responsible and that they are touchy and easily irritated. It is not necessary to get angry with such horses; in fact this may easily just make them bad tempered. If they are merely lodging an objection to the girth or the roller, then it is best to soothe and coax them to be sweeter tempered by gentle handling.

Only when the horse really tries to kick you should he be reprimanded, and then it must be done very firmly. The risk of serious injury from a well-placed kick must be avoided; you must take a firm line with horses who kick and mean it. This does not mean that they should not still be handled gently. If treated roughly, they may become more vicious, so you will need to develop a friendship with them, coupled with a healthy respect. Never stand at arm's length when grooming or rugging up, as you will make a fine target at such a distance. The closer you stand, the less likely the horse will be able to take a decent swing at you. If you are frightened, you probably will be kicked, as the horse will instinctively know and try to take advantage of the situation.

You must be bold with him and talk to him calmly and quietly. If he begins to lay his ears back and swish his tail or lift his hind feet, a sharp change in your tone of voice will warn him that you know what he is thinking and that you will get angry too. Remind him of his position in the 'pecking order' (*see* page 9) that is, below you, and that you are in control.

Biting

Horses who bite are generally unhappy creatures and such aggression is their way of showing their discontentment; but like all bad habits it will get worse if not dealt with when it first arises. Biting is recognized as a vice.

It is natural for horses to bite each other, both in play as youngsters and in earnest when adult; and just as puppies and kittens have to be taught not to bite and scratch, the young horse has to be taught not to bite and kick us even in play. All young horses will nip occasionally; this must never be allowed to pass uncorrected, even if it is only a display of high spirits. A tap on the muzzle and a sharp 'no' is sufficient to teach the youngster not to be cheeky; letting him get away with it will only encourage him to do it again.

Carrying titbits or pony nuts in the pockets of clothing is asking for trouble as it will encourage horses to nibble at you to get at them. When they 'ask' in this way, they will naturally be annoyed if they know you have titbits in your pocket and may well try to bite when you suddenly refuse them if they are used to being given them.

Rough grooming or careless handling of highly strung or thin-skinned horses is bound to make them show their objection; and if you are the cause of the horse's discontentment, he may well grab you in his teeth. When a horse shows he is upset by swishing his tail and pulling faces you must take care to see that he is not upset further; if his threats are not heeded they will progress and worsen.

There are occasions when a horse is justified in trying to bite his handler, especially if he is being subjected to unnecessary annoyance through his handler's thoughtlessness. Continued thoughtlessness coupled with unfair punishment for trying to bite will soon make him very bad tempered.

Riding school horses and ponies often suffer from being continually disturbed, i.e., for grooming, tacking-up, untacking, etc., and some of them adopt threatening expressions to ward people away from themselves, especially when they are trying to rest. Any horse who wears a miserable expression on his face when you walk into his box is obviously not happy with his lot and it can take a very long time to change his attitude.

As mentioned above, correct management of the young horse teaches him to keep his teeth to himself. However, if his subsequent life style as an adult horse is unpleasant, he will become a misery to look after. If you have just bought such a horse, you will want to get on good terms with him, and want him to enjoy belonging to you.

If a horse is a really vicious biter, he should be muzzled for the protection of those who have to handle him; fortunately, really mean horses are seldom found these days, since they are better cared for now than in the past when they were often treated like working machines. Most horses who bite these days do so for the reasons mentioned above.

When being groomed or mucked out, they should be tied up short enough to prevent them from being able to bite. They should however, be talked to, soothed, and handled considerately so that they learn to enjoy your presence in the stable. They should be disturbed as little as possible and allowed peace and quiet. Never try grooming at feed time (*see* page 37), as this is bound to be irritating and will compound the problem. It may be wise to keep the horse's headcollar on at all times, so that when you enter the stable, you can catch him without risking being bitten before you have him under control.

If he bites at people passing the stable door, he should never be struck or threatened, as he will probably hurt his head trying to avoid being hit, and could become headshy – albeit through his own fault. If possible, he should be moved to a box where the yard is less busy so that he will not be passed so often. A warning notice on the stable door will make people give him a wide berth. It is a shame to put up a grille and stop him from looking out, as he is already a bit of a misery, and it will not improve his outlook on life. If he must live in the middle of a busy yard, he is better off wearing a muzzle, but he should still be avoided as much as possible so that he is not annoyed, and of course, he must never be teased or baited.

Each time he tries to bite when you are grooming or tacking-up etc., say 'no' loudly to him and then lower your voice and soothe him. Do not raise a hand to him, even to push his head away, as this will only give him a target for his teeth to aim at. Only if he actually makes contact with his teeth should he have a slap on the nose. In time he will learn that you are his friend and if you handle him fairly and considerately, he should enjoy your being near him. He will also find out that if he does bite you, you will retaliate by slapping him and he should eventually give up trying to bite you.

8 Handling and loading difficulties

Headshyness

Being headshy is neither a vice nor a bad habit, but a state of mind; it is nonetheless a serious problem and deserves a place here. Most often, it results from unsympathetic, thoughtless handling and being hit about the head so frequently that eventually the horse expects to be hit every time a hand is raised near him, at which he will toss his head violently and may jump back to avoid being struck. Great sympathy, understanding and patience will be needed, coupled with soft words and plenty of time, if the horse is to regain his confidence in man.

A headshy horse is often difficult to handle because he tends to panic easily. Although he can be very trying, for a handler to lose his temper with him is an admission of failure. A horse should *never* be struck about the head, for any reason whatsoever. The only time he should even be given a slap on the muzzle is if he attempts to bite, and then it must be done cautiously and carefully. If a horse starts nibbling at your pockets or clothing, you need only push his head away and say 'no!' loudly. If after a couple of times he persists, then move out of his way but do not be tempted to hit him. Carrying pony nuts in coat pockets only encourages this nibbling which can lead to biting, as can the regular giving of titbits. Both these habits should be avoided.

When working around the headshy horse, every movement made towards him must be slow and deliberate, especially at grooming or rugging-up time. Brushing around the head itself may be out of the question; to begin with, a folded soft cloth should be used to gently stroke the cheeks and nose only. Although the horse will need to be tied up for grooming, care must be taken not to make him pull back (*see* page 24), especially when attending to the face and neck areas.

When rugging up, do not try to throw the rugs over in the usual

90

way. Have them ready folded and place them quietly on the horse's back and then arrange them, talking quietly to him as you go.

Great care should be taken when putting on his headcollar or bridle. To begin with, it may help to leave his headcollar on all the time, so you can avoid the possibility of upsetting him every time you need to catch him, even when he is in the stable.

If he will not let you bridle him in the usual way, take the noseband off the bridle altogether, then undo the nearside cheekpiece at the bit, and slip it out from the browband. Do not try to put the reins over his head to begin with, but unbuckle them at the hand part and pass the offside one around his neck and fasten it to the nearside one at the wither. Then pass the headpiece around and over his neck in the same way so that you can slide the bridle up into place from behind his ears. Pass the headpiece back through the browband loop and ask the horse to accept the bit. When it is in his mouth, fasten the

It may help with a headshy horse to leave a headcollar on all the time for a while. An adjustable nylon one like this is strong, durable and cheaper than a leather one; it can be made to fit most horses.

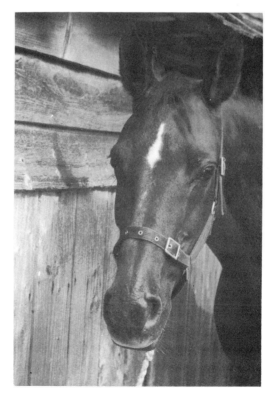

cheekpiece back onto it. Obviously this procedure must be carried out slowly and carefully and the horse reassured and calmed. In time, it will hopefully be possible to bridle him in the normal way, but do not hurry him.

In the early stages, the more time you can spend with the horse the better; and eventually, with gentle handling, he will come round. Although it may take a long time in bad cases, it is very rewarding to build up a strong bond of trust and friendship with a horse, especially one whose initial attitude was one of fear and mistrust.

Shoeing
Good farriers are sometimes hard to come by, and they will be able to pick and choose their clients. No farrier wants to shoe a horse who is liable to hurt him, as his livelihood depends on his fitness and ability to carry out his work. It is therefore very important that your horse stands quietly and behaves himself when being shod, or your farrier might well refuse to continue shoeing him.

Like many bad habits, misbehaving whilst being shod may be the result of incorrect handling of the horse as a youngster. Foals and youngstock should be taught to pick up their feet properly when asked. They should have them picked out regularly in any case, and it is essential that they have learned to do this before the farrier is expected to deal with them.

If you breed your own stock, it is sensible to have your farrier handle the foal when the mare's feet need to be dressed. Even if the foal's feet do not need trimming, he needs to get used to the farrier's smoky 'aroma' which may frighten him to begin with; fear of fire and smoke is a natural instinct that must be overcome before the horse will settle to being shod. While he is still small and impressionable, he should learn not to fear the farrier, and should meet him several times before he actually needs to be shod as a young strong adult horse. Youngsters should have their feet attended to regularly to keep them in good order, and it is a good preparation for the day when they will need their first set of shoes.

When the time comes for the young horse to be actually shod, he must not be tied up to begin with, but held by someone whom he knows and trusts. If the youngster has been well handled and is used to being obedient, naturally he will be far less trouble that if he has not had proper training. Also, the farrier is more likely to be gentle and patient with him if he behaves reasonably well. It may also be a good idea to have him cold shod on the first few occasions as then there will be no smoke to upset him; the whole experience will be new to him, so it is better to go through it in stages. Hot shoeing should, however, be introduced at a later date; it is preferable to cold shoeing, because the shoes will be a better fit and the weight distribution will be absolutely equal right around the wall of the foot if they are burned on.

The young horse should be held firmly in position so that the farrier can shoe him, but should be soothed if he is frightened, and gently persuaded, rather than forced, to stand still. A bowl of nuts may help to keep his mind off his worries.

Very few horses actually fear being shod on account of having experienced pain, as it is extremely rare for a farrier accidently to 'prick' the sensitive part of the foot when driving in a nail; this only happens if the horse moves sharply, just as the farrier is using his hammer. However, fear of smoke may persist in adult life in highly-strung horses and for them cold shoeing may be the only answer.

With the older horse, good manners are to be expected, and are of paramount importance. The farrier will usually be able to deal with the horse and make him mind his manners, but biting or kicking must never be allowed. It is up to the handler to hold the horse steady and see that he cannot take a bite out of the farrier; no one could expect a farrier to shoe a horse that continually tried to kick. If the problem is sheer disobedience, it may be necessary to use the twitch when the hind feet are being done; after a few occasions, once the horse has learned that he must stand still and behave, it may be possible to dispense with it.

There is a fast growing trend these days to ride horses unshod, due to the ever-increasing financial outlay of shoes. If you are considering this, it is important to know what is involved in doing it satisfactorily.

Horses in their natural environment can choose where they put their feet and will avoid moving fast over hard and rough terrain except in emergency. On the other hand, the domesticated horse has to tread where he is told, which may be on stony ground and hard road surfaces. These will wear down the feet, and can cause severe bruising if care is not taken. You can judge how much wear will take place to your own horse's feet if you ride him unshod, by the amount of wear to his shoes that takes place, bearing in mind of course, that his shoes are much more durable than the horn that he can grow.

Roadwork wears the feet very quickly, and stepping on stones or gravel at the kerbside will cause bruising. Stepping on stones on soft earth will not bruise the sole though, as the stone itself will sink into the soil and not be pressed hard up into the foot. If you wish to ride your horse unshod, you will have to allow his feet to grow out a little and harden off, so that he gets used to it once the shoes have been removed; much in the same way as if you wished to go barefoot yourself, you would have to let the skin harden on the soles of your feet before you could run around happily. Remember that it takes between nine and fifteen months for a horse's foot to grow out completely from the coronary band to the ground, and this period of time will differ greatly from horse to horse, according to his ration of feed and general well-being. You can however, stimulate this growth rate by applying a proprietary paste such as 'Cornucrescine' twice daily to the coronary band, which holds the horn-producing cells. 'Cornucrescine' is in fact, a very mild blister, and promotes good blood circulation which will assist the growth rate. It is a good idea to start this treatment about one month before the shoes are to be taken off, and it may be reduced to once a day thereafter.

Obviously the amount and type of work you can do with an unshod horse will differ greatly from that of the shod horse. Road work will be very wearing to the feet, as will riding on any kind of rough or hard ground. If you can only ride at weekends, you should have no trouble if you choose where you ride very carefully, especially to begin with. Of course, you will not be able to work the horse six days a week or hunt him unshod; and jumping and competing necessitate the wearing of studs, which require him to be shod.

Even if you are successful in managing without shoes, watch out for cracks and splits developing which may damage the feet. The farrier will be required from time to time, to trim them if they occur. Including cod liver oil in the horse's diet will also promote good growth of the horn and regular use of a good hoof oil will be necessary to keep feet in good condition.

Fear of veterinary examination

Horses have a highly developed sense of smell and veterinary surgeons generally have a clinical aroma about them. Most horses only see the vet when they are being examined for lameness, cuts and other painful reasons, and may soon begin to connect the aroma with

94

the pain to be suffered even from the most gentle examination. Also, a number of horses share an instinctive fear of the smell of pigs; if perchance the vet has just come from a pig farm, possibly the smell of pigs may be carried with him on his boots or clothing. This could explain any unexpected nervous behaviour or lack of co-operation on the part of a horse who is usually quite amenable.

Generally, horses who are frightened when being handled by the vet react in one of two ways – they either struggle to get away and become unmanageable, or, less commonly, they actually put up an aggressive fight. Obviously, the veterinary surgeon, in common with the farrier, will not take kindly to being put out of action by an obstreperous horse. If the horse concerned is known to be difficult to handle and likely to rear or strike out, a twitch may be advisable and should be put on before the horse is examined.

It should not be necessary, nor is it in fact advisable, to ask the vet to examine the horse out in the open, unless he has to be trotted up during examination for lameness; but it is important that any stable used for examination purposes has sufficient light for the vet to see. It should also have enough headroom, so that if the horse rears he will not risk hitting his head. If assistance is needed in handling the horse and there is no one suitable on hand, then it is best to advise the vet when asking him to attend, so he can bring an assistant with him if possible.

A difficult problem arises with horses who will not stand for injections. While your horse may not need any other treatment throughout the year, he must have annual anti-tetanus and equine influenza vaccination boosters. As it is now possible to have these two vaccines given in the one dose, instead of two separate injections as before, the chances of actually getting the job done are much improved. By being well organized before the vet arrives, you may be able to achieve this using the following method, for this one occasion each year.

Probably the best place to put your horse for this treatment is in a double horse trailer. If you do not own one, try to borrow one. Load the horse before the vet arrives so during loading he will be more calm than if the vet were present, and to avoid wasting the vet's time in case he proves a problem to load (*see* page 96). He should be bandaged for travelling, and wear a poll protector, knee caps and hock boots if possible. There must also be a generous amount of bedding on the trailer floor, and straw bales in front of the breast bar, for the horse's protection. The handler should be armed with a bucket with some oats in it; if it is possible for the horse to wear some form of makeshift blinkers, without getting upset, so much the better. If this is not possible, the handler should cover the horse's eyes so that he cannot see what is going on behind him when the time comes for the injection.

He should be tied up securely and wear a nylon headcollar.

The vet should enter the trailer by the groom door with the syringe at the ready, and, standing in the spare space, with the partition between him and the horse, give the injection in the hindquarters as quickly and quietly as possible. With any luck, it will have been successfully given before the horse can do anything about it; if he does erupt, he should not damage himself or any one else if he has been properly prepared. The vet should then vacate the trailer, and the horse be soothed and fed oats until calm.

The one drawback with this 'surprise' method is that it could make the horse difficult to load if he starts to suspect the arrival of the vet; but as it is only necessary to use it very occasionally, and then with skill and speed, this should not happen. The horse's confidence can be restored with careful handling, hopefully without too much trouble. It is really a small risk to run against the much greater risks of the horse contracting either tetanus, which can prove fatal, or equine influenza, which can damage the wind for life.

Loading into a horsebox or trailer

A horse who is difficult to load into a horsebox or trailer can cause a good deal of distress to himself, and great inconvenience to his owner. To begin with, let us consider it from his point of view.

Having been in one of those things before, he knows that it is dark inside, noisy, terribly bumpy and he cannot see out. It is easy for him to lose his balance. If he travels next to a horse who has not been tied up sufficiently short, he can spend the whole journey being bullied. The headroom is usually low so he can bang his head, and every time the driver has to stop sharply, he hurts his shoulders and chest on the breast bar. If his tail has not been bandaged, it can be badly rubbed even on a short journey. So your horse may have suffered both physically and mentally whilst being transported and you cannot help sympathizing with him. How can anyone really expect him to go into the box without a fuss if he has been subjected to any or all of these discomforts in the past?

His objections will probably range from a stubborn stance at the bottom of the ramp to a rearing, kicking horse who will drag his handler as far away from the box as possible, and refuse to return anywhere near it.

Driving a horsebox or trailer correctly

The actual way you drive a horsebox or trailer has an enormous effect on the attitude of the horse towards being loaded into it. So you must drive in a way which causes minimum discomfort and stress. Horses who are travelled badly and carelessly become bad loaders, so it is worth taking extreme care.

The horses cannot see out of the box and do not know which way it will turn next, or when it will stop and start. They have the constant problem of balancing so must be driven slowly and carefully. Remember that horses do not step sideways easily or naturally, so their balance is more hampered than you realize. Speed needs to be considered carefully, for although it may be safe to travel at 65 kph (40 mph) when using the motorway where there is no interfering traffic, an emergency stop from as little as 24 kph (15 mph) can be a frightening experience for the horses.

Cornering is most unbalancing of all and, in Britain, on roundabouts particularly. Even when one intends to go straight across, this involves a swing to the left, followed immediately by a swing to the right, followed again by a swing to the left. Never hurry along even if you are late. If traffic is building up behind the box, it is better to stop and let it pass and then set off again. Always keep well back from other vehicles, so that if they stop suddenly, you will not have to brake hard.

If horses are travelled intelligently and carefully, they should never become bad travellers or bad to load. Not doing so is the most common cause of the problem.

There is another reason, and that is the purpose of the journey. If your horse enjoys what he does when he gets out of the box at the destination – for example, a good day's hunting – he will associate travelling with enjoyment, and may even sweat up in the excitement of anticipation. If on the other hand, he goes to shows regularly, to be jumped and shown in every possible class in the heat of the summer and thoroughly exhausted by the proceedings, it will not be long before he associates travelling with another ghastly day, and will become difficult to load.

Preparations and clothing for travelling

Great care must also be taken in preparing a horse for travelling (*see* photograph page 79). His legs must be carefully bandaged with stable bandages, which must have sufficient gamgee underneath them to cover the coronary band, important in case the horse loses his balance and treads on himself, when he may badly damage the horn-producing coronary band, or at least lame himself temporarily. Such pain inflicted in the box will also add to any fear of travelling that he may already have. It should be noted that bandages must be applied anti-clockwise to the nearside legs and clockwise to the off-side legs. This is to make sure that no strain is placed on the tendons which would result if the legs were not bandaged in the correct way. This is particularly important when applying exercise bandages for support during fast work as bandaging the wrong way would only weaken the leg rather than support it.

Bandaging of the tail, as mentioned, is important because with trailer ramps especially, the tail can get badly rubbed; horses often use the ramp to lean on for support and the swaying back and forth will soon rub them raw. A leather tail-guard over the bandage affords the best protection and will ensure that the bandage does not become dislodged, particularly on longer journeys.

Kneecaps are important for loading and unloading: a fall on the ramp can cause extensive damage to the knees. It is very easy for a horse to slip and fall on a wet ramp and the price of a pair of kneecaps is money well spent if you travel your horse regularly. Hock boots are not usually necessary for ponies, but are of great value to large horses who may bang their hocks on account of their closeness to the partition or ramp behind them.

Make sure that your horse is wearing enough blankets to be warm in winter, but remember that a box full of steaming horses returning from hunting can quickly overheat the inside. The reverse is true of open-backed trailers and it is important to keep the horses warm enough, so that they do not catch a chill if they have to be travelled before cooling off properly.

Poll-protectors can be purchased to fit on to the headpiece of the headcollar, and are the especially advantageous to big horses. They will reduce the force of a blow to the top of the horse's head if it hits the roof of the trailer.

Make sure that the roller or surcingle which hold the rugs in place is sufficiently tight to stop the rugs from slipping, and never be tempted to leave it off, even if your horse is only wearing an anti-sweat sheet. This could easily slip round underneath before very long and in any case would be ruined under the horse's feet. It is also likely to make him panic.

Your horse should be tied up quite short in the box or trailer. This will keep him facing fairly straight, which will assist his balance, and give him support. If two horses travel side by side, they should be tied up so that cannot bite or bully one another. Always use a quick-release knot when tying up for travelling, and always tie a piece of binder twine or something similar between the tie-ring and the rope. If the rope is tied directly to the tie-ring and there is an accident or the horse falls down, the rope will tighten and be hard to release. Under such pressure, the twine should break, and even if it does not, it will be easier to cut through than a rope. (*See* page 25.)

Sufficient bedding must also be provided for the horses to stand on, so that in case they slip or fall the risk of injury will be minimized. It is most important to keep the floors of boxes and trailers clean and dry, because if wet bedding is left there it will rot the wooden floors and rust away the metal below. The results could then prove fatal one day.

Loading a naughty horse
Some horses obviously are not frightened at all, but still play up and refuse to go in. In these cases, you may persuade the horse with the aid of some oats or nuts in a feed bowl and if you have an assistant handy, he may be well employed in applying a little 'strong-arm' technique from behind (assuming that the horse may be trusted not to kick). Sometimes the assistant's voice and a slap or two on the rump will suffice, but if not, you can try the following technique.

This method of loading a horse requires three intelligent and reasonably strong people who must be well-used to horses so they have the 'know-how' to help. The horse must be wearing a bridle over his headcollar so that his leader has a good degree of control. He should be bandaged (including his tail) and if possible, wear kneecaps to prevent knee injuries in case he falls on the ramp, or indeed off it.

Two lunge lines or long ropes will be needed, attached to either side of the box at the back, at a height of not less than 1.2m (4ft) from the ground. One assistant will be leading the horse and the other two should hold one line each, straight outwards from the back of the trailer (*see* photograph page 79 above) keeping them well off the ground to prevent them getting caught up in the horse's legs. The horse is then led straight up the lane between the two lunge lines. When the horse's rump has passed the two line assistants, they quickly change sides behind the horse, criss-crossing the lines at the level of the horse's second thighs (*see* photograph page 79 below). These two lines must be kept taut as the assistants then both move towards the box with the horse, taking up the slack and keeping the tension even on each side.

Should the horse resist, it is most important that the lines are dropped, as his legs may rapidly become entangled in them. It is the responsibility of the leader to try to keep the horse straight, but if he tries to rear or whip round, watch out that he does not hurt himself, or for that matter, his handlers. It is also important for the leader to stand facing the box. Never stand facing a horse when you are trying to load him, as it will put him off.

Now repeat the process as before, calmly and quietly. If after several attempts you find that you are getting nowhere, use your experience to judge whether a couple of smart slaps will be expedient, to make sure the horse knows you mean business. This may be the answer, but patience may win through without the use of force and if it is possible, so much the better.

If you can, park the box alongside a wall, as this will reduce the number of escape routes open to the horse. Ideally, a suitable passageway to park in is enormously helpful, but you will not always find one handy, especially for the homeward journey.

Most naughty horses can be loaded successfully by the above method, but it is a process which can only work if it is executed with firmness and competence. Remember also that many horses will enter horseboxes but not trailers, because of the headroom, or rather lack of it. This usually occurs with horses over fifteen hands high. The golden rule is never to pull on the lead rope, as this makes the horse raise his head and then he will realize that the ceiling is low. This also usually happens before the horse has even reached the highest part of the ramp, so all is lost before you begin. While the leader keeps the horse straight, the pressure from the lunge lines behind will edge him forward. The leader can encourage the horse to keep his head down by having a bowl of oats or nuts in one hand. This can be used to tempt him along and he should only be allowed to eat from it when he has made some progress.

Loading a frightened horse

The horse who exhibits true fear of horseboxes and trailers requires different handling altogether. A more lengthy operation will definitely be necessary before a cure can be effected, which will certainly not be on the morning of the show when the problem is first discovered! If you own your own horsebox or trailer, or can borrow one for a while, you are half-way to solving the problem. You must however, have the time and patience necessary before you embark upon this cure, or you will not succeed and your horse will probably end up worse than before.

Park the box in a suitable place, preferably in a small paddock or fenced area and leave the ramp down. On the first day, it there are other horses in the yard, feed them, but not your problem horse. Put his breakfast near the ramp of the box. If you have two sets of brushing boots and a pair of kneecaps, then put these on; they should provide all the protection he needs to begin with. Put on his headcollar and lead him to the rear of the box where his feed is waiting. It is hoped that on the first attempt you should be able to coax your horse to eat his breakfast with the feed tin on the ramp of the box, which he should willingly do, unless he is petrified. Your first aim during this method is to have your horse associate the box with being rewarded. With kind words and coaxing you may even succeed in getting him to eat his feed with his front feet half-way up the ramp on the first occasion. You may even persuade him to go right into the box; but if you are so fortunate, do not attempt to tie him up. If he took fright and ran back, he could break his headcollar, probably hit his head on the roof, shoot down the ramp backwards terrified, and certainly be thoroughly frightened, if not hurt. It would ruin your chances of ever loading him again so easily. The same applies to having someone try to put up the ramp, should he oblige and go into the box. The last thing you want to do is make him panic, or feel that he has been trapped, and the more time you can take at this stage, the better will be your final result. So leave the ramp down for now.

If you are lucky enough to get him right into the box and he then backs out, be quick to allow him to do so and go quietly with him, talking soothingly to him. At this stage, make no attempt to stop him by pulling on the rope, as he must be given freedom of choice if you are to gain his confidence. Ignore the incident as though it had not occurred, and when he is settled, gently try to persuade him to eat some more of his feed and enter the box if he will. Any attempt to apply physical or mental pressure at this stage will overcome his will to co-operate, and spoil any progress you have made. The essence of success is kindness, patience and the time necessary to effect a proper cure; this cannot be overstressed.

You can repeat this procedure every feed time or once a day, depending on the amount of time you can afford. Remember that once you have associated the box as a place where your horse is fed and rewarded, he will look forward to going into it, but do be sure that he is going in and out quite happily before you have someone shut the ramp. When he is completely at ease in the box you can attempt to take him for a journey.

When the day arrives that you decide to take him out in the box, you will need someone to drive for you, on this and his first few outings. You yourself must travel in the box with your horse to reassure him, feed him and be ready to signal to the driver to stop if necessary. The first journey should be kept quite short – ten minutes will be long enough. If you are able to travel another good quiet horse on these practice runs, so much the better; the influence of another calm horse beside him will be reassuring.

Recent research in the USA suggests that horses travel more happily facing the rear of a trailer or box, because this is more comfortable physically. This cannot be done in a conventional trailer, nor should it be attempted, but trailers designed for horses to face the rear are now on the market.

Glossary of US equivalents

Britain	USA
back at the knee	calf-kneed
bandages	leg wraps
barking foal	barker
broken wind	heaves
brushing	interfering
caul	sac
cracked heel	scratches; greased heel
cubes	pellets
field	paddock
fortnight	two weeks
girth	cinch; girth
good doer	good keeper
hacking; riding out	pleasure riding; trail riding
halt (long distance rides)	check point
halter	rope halter
headcollar	halter
horse box	van
laminitis	founder
loose box	box stall
lorry	truck
lucerne	alfalfa
maize	corn
nettlerash	hives
numnah	saddle pad
nuts, cubes	pellets

offset cannons	bench knees
on a sixpence	on a dime
over at the knee	calf-kneed
overreach boots	bell boots
paddock	corral
pervious urachus	persistent urachus
plaits	braids
rasp teeth or hooves	float teeth or hooves
rein back	back
remove shoes	reset shoes
rise to the trot	post
rosette	ribbons
rug, rugging	blanket, blanketing
sack	feed bag
show schedules	prize lists
sleepy foal	sleeper
society; organization	conference
stable rubber	stable towel
stirrup treads	stirrup pads
tarred road	black top
travel a horse	truck a horse
wind galls	wind puffs